Black Sonshine

A Guide for Raising Black Males into Intelligent,
Well-Adjusted Men in the 21st Century.

Dr. Terrance Wells

Copyright © 2023

Dr. Terrance Wells

Print ISBN:

979-8-218-16816-2

Library of Congress Control Number:

2023904575

Contents

Black Sonshine

A Guide for Raising Black Males into Intelligent, Well-Adjusted Men in the 21st Century.

Dr. Terrance Wells

Dedication

I dedicate this body of work to my loving mother and father, Margaret and Houlson Wells Jr. I also dedicate this to my four children, Daschae, Tnai, Terrance Jr., Omari, and grandchildren now and to come. Special thanks to my siblings, Brenda, Derrick, Dawan, and Sydney. Also, a special thanks goes out to my clinical supervisor and mentor Dr. Juenerral Keith. Finally, I dedicate this book to my loving wife, LaKeisha, who has supported me and devoted her life to me as I have devoted mine to her. To my family and friends, I thank you all sincerely for having the audacity to believe in me!

A Note From the Author

I sincerely thank you for taking the time to allow me to share information regarding a subject that is near and dear to me. It is my desire to uplift and educate those that seek knowledge and have a desire to reach their full potential as an individual caregiver or educator. This body of work will cover a wide spectrum of knowledge utilizing research, psychology, history, theory and real life experiences. These elements previously mentioned will provide insight and awareness regarding the current issues affecting black males in America. I sincerely hope you are not only informed but empowered by this humble offering.

Black Sonshine

*L*et your light shine before men, that they may see your good works and glorify the father.

(Matthew 5:14-16).

You never know, there might be somebody down in the valley trying to get home. God Bless you!

Introduction

*B*lack *Sonshine.* I selected this title because of the process it takes to cultivate a precious jewel. During the early stages, a jewel must be taken out of the earth and undergo an intensive, meticulous process. All the imperfections must be chipped and ground away before it can become something valuable. It must undergo years of processing and polishing to bring about a shine that can illuminate the world. Once the jewel reaches its final form, we can only describe its illuminating beauty in a single word: flawless.

This metaphor is likened to raising Black boys into manhood. Remember, manhood is not a phenomenon that can be put in a box like a jewel. It is a dynamic, ever-evolving experience that only men can understand after they have reached an age of maturity. Like the jewel, a man must go through a series of stages before he can exhibit value in his personal and professional life. It is no longer enough to feed, clothe, discipline, and teach a system of morality as it once was in the past. While those elements are necessary, it does not equip them with what they need in the 21st century. The world is different now and will require more of a hands-on, cognitive approach to parenting, because of all the information and traps that so many Black males fall victim to. This manual will not only teach helpful strategies that have been proven to be effective within my practice as a psychologist, but it has also assisted me in the development of rearing my three sons who are currently 28, 17, and 14 years old.

As a social scientist with over twenty-six years of specializing in working with Black males within the counseling profession, I have some serious concerns that must be addressed within our community. I have noticed an increase in negative trends that influence the quality of life for Black males and how their personalities are developed. I am sure that you are aware of the issues that plague our males, such as high incarceration rates, homicide, poor academic performance, suicide, absent fathers, and low life expectancies, to name a few.

These are symptoms of a greater issue that lies within our inability to equip Black males with the tools necessary to make sound decisions when faced with trials and harsh realities. It appears we have become numb to some of the social illnesses that affect our males. Social illnesses and dysfunction have become a subculture of their own by promoting ignorance and self-destructive behaviors. After years of working with Black males and their families, it has been my mission to help a population that has been the most hated, despised, and traumatized above all others. I am determined to help them heal so they can become whole. I have been effective in treating people from all walks of life; however, I have been compelled to specialize in working with Black males of African descent.

This has been my ministry and calling in which I have had to answer. Within the counseling profession, there is a degree of suffering being experienced by the helper or therapist that compels them to dedicate their life to service. I have hoped to be the support for others; I wish I had as a Black adolescent male experiencing my trials and tribulations.

Through sacrifice and diligence, God has used me to help others, and I hope to help many more through this humble offering of my thoughts toward a sensitive subject.

This book will achieve five goals:

1) Assist you in learning about the psychological development of Black males in America.

2) Assist in the development of using effective parenting strategies for Black males.

3) Combat many of the vicious assaults waged against Black males.

4) Educate and equip Black males with the tools necessary to survive and thrive in America.

5) Provide new therapeutic interventions that are useful in working with males of African descent.

Parenting is one of the most challenging jobs an individual might have in this world. It will test you on every level imaginable for the rest of your life. Now, let us complicate things by adding into the equation the responsibility of parenting a Black male in America. The mere thought is scary and will require you to learn new information and be ever so vigilant in your observations, interventions, and ongoing support. The information you learn may very well be the one piece of knowledge that can save your son's life.

Color Classification of Race

Because of the negative connotations that come along with calling our young boys Black males, I will discontinue doing so within this body of work. The color codes of classifying people within American society are deeply rooted in white supremacy. In fact, America became a melting pot for people that could pass as being White. For example, those who were Greek, German, Irish, Russian, or French could come to the new world and be classified as White because of their fairer complexion. Those desirable immigrants could receive social privileges and economic incentives so they could benefit from a country built by those who were enslaved.

This color classification came with rights and privileges, giving them advantages over those who were nonwhite, especially those who were labeled as Black. Within the societal power structure, the color classification of "White" is considered superior, while "Black" is considered inferior. Therefore, giving someone the title of "male" when coupled with the word "Black" has a negative connotation because it simply refers to a biological classification that can be shared with animals or any other living creature. If you truly think about it, the term dehumanizes a group and provides no context for history or culture.

Kingship Restored

From this moment on, I will refer to our young men as being young kings or a male of African descent. The title of male of African descent is self-explanatory; however, kingship was purposefully granted because our identity and culture have been stripped away and must be rediscovered. A king is the most important member of a royal family and one who is expected to lead, protect, and govern. These attributes are needed to build strong family systems and reclaim our heritage. These titles identify us as originating from a land mass known for its rich culture and birthing all civilizations. In the words of Dr. Henry Clark, "Before colonialism in Africa, there wasn't a name for a jail, orphanage, or nursing home because we came from great people who governed themselves and civilized the world."

The psychological development of males of African descent is a topic that has not been thoroughly researched because of our tendency to view psychology from a European perspective. The African American experience is unlike any other in America and has been heavily scrutinized by others to define our identity. My intention is to bring light to this topic so that caregivers, parents, and even their children can create a new reality in which the young king is put into a position to be successful in life and reach their full potential.

As prestigious as the name young kings is, the journey of these young men is nowhere near glamorous. The road which these young men must travel will be filled with traps and snares that other cultural groups will never have to deal with. Therefore, I believe every male of African descent in America should be considered at risk because of all the systems designed to emasculate and eliminate them. I often describe being a Black man in America like wearing a long, weighted, black coat.

The coat you have been gifted with since birth. No matter how much you have achieved in this world or how much money you have amassed, you will quickly be reminded that you are still a Black man in America. This reminder most often comes from those who wear the black coat as well. The acknowledgment of this reality is not an attempt to "throw shade," but simply to warn you of what will occur if you ever forget. The wearing of this coat is heavily laden with pain, struggle, and fear; despite that, we rise.

There is so much that has been lost along the way that must be rediscovered. We will not waste time focusing on the problem. It is my goal to teach caregivers how to implement strategies and techniques that will equip our young kings with the skills to become responsible, well-adjusted men. As parents, we have been chosen to develop a human being from birth throughout life. To effectively parent a young king in America, our awareness and understanding must expand.

We must understand what is going on in this world so we can pass knowledge on to our children, who need it most. Our lives can get so busy, and we forget to give our young kings the tools needed to not only survive but flourish. Many parents are so engulfed with their personal challenges, they often miss opportunities to take advantage of those critical stages of their child's development. As caregivers, we should learn the basics of early childhood development and have a strategic plan on how we wish to cultivate them.

Early Childhood Development

Within this book, we will explore the stages of development of males of African descent from birth through young adulthood to provide insight into current trends. The Greek philosopher Aristotle once said, "Give me a child until he is 7, and I will show you the man." Ages 0-7 are considered the super learning stages of a child's development. During this time, your child's mind is like a sponge that will absorb any information provided and is consistently reinforced. In essence, your child is like a canvas, and you have an opportunity to assist them in painting a masterpiece.

From a biological standpoint, these early years are when children spend most of their time in alpha and theta brain wave cycles, which is like a state of hypnosis or meditation. So, if you could, imagine your child walking around in a state of hypnosis, absorbing everything they encounter. This is one reason infants need naps; they are being flooded with information and stimulation, which promotes the development of the brain. Between the ages of 2-3, the child pretend plays and engages in imaginary fantasies. Pretend play may appear as mere childish games; however, they stimulate creativity, thinking, and social skills.

Ironically, as a child around age 5 years old, I can recall taking part in imaginary games. I remember sharing vivid stories with my peers. While sharing my stories, my playmates would often inquire by asking, "For real?" and my response would typically be, "No, for Play-Play." Play-Play or make-believe is a game in which children go back and forth by telling stories and role-playing. This "make-believe" stage is very important because they are not only playing but are being programmed by their experiences and their environments. During these stages, parents should focus on providing structure and teaching emotional intelligence, effective communication, and introducing positive stories and themes.

These four elements will provide a firm foundation in which you will introduce positive programming that promotes confidence and a positive self-concept. This will require you to censor all information and expose young kings to positive experiences. Your child is learning and picking up on everything at this stage of their life. Everything you say, do, and expose them to will be a part of who they grow up to be. As a parent who is aware of this, it's your responsibility to only allow them access to information that will help them in their development, not hinder it.

When a child is around eight years old, he will develop the sphere of his brain called the prefrontal cortex, which is responsible for critical thinking, reasoning, problem-solving, impulse control, creativity, and perseverance. This stage is critical as well because this is the time in which the child develops a self-concept. Not only are they being exposed to different stimuli, but they also are deciding how they will use the things they have been exposed to differentiate themselves from others. Young kings become more independent and explore, which is often perceived as being disobedient because of their curiosity and high energy levels.

Why do young kings lose interest in school?

Historically, around the third grade is when a young king's academic performance and test scores decline drastically. The reason may shock you. Dr. Jawanza Kunjufu, a renowned educator, coined the term "fourth-grade failure syndrome" to explain why most young males of African descent decline at this grade level. The educational and social decline among young kings becomes more prevalent as they mature. Parents and educators have less influence in their lives, and the media and peers become the dominant force in their development. This causes a shift in which more emphasis is placed on being cool and playing sports rather than learning.

Within this stage, the male that is cool or athletically inclined receives positive reinforcement and is rewarded by his peers. Unfortunately, being cool and athletic will take priority over being smart and well-behaved. This causes poor academic performance, which leads to disciplinary issues. I believe we must strengthen all positive supports so that our young kings can *avoid* these negative influences, but also be aware of the *consequences* of the distractions. I have conducted countless surveys of young kings between the ages of 8 and 13 inquiring about what they want to be when they grow up. About 80% of them would respond by selecting an occupation in sports or entertainment. This is troubling when you consider that only 1.2% of college-level players will get drafted into the NFL, and the probability of playing professional basketball is even lower. Only 0.02 to 0.03 percent of high school players will be drafted to the NBA. That means only around 2-3 will be drafted out of 10,000 high school players. As adults, we know these are not realistic career choices for many of our young kings, and many will change their career goals once reality sets in.

To be clear, I am not saying you shouldn't support young kings in pursuing their dream or ignore their gift if they are a talented athlete or entertainer. However, I am saying there can only be one Ja Morant, Michael Jordan, and LeBron James. Those extraordinary athletes previously mentioned not only made ultimate sacrifices in training, but they also were born with an extraordinary genetic advantage. For example, many people use Michael Jordan's story of being cut from the team in high school as proof that his work ethic and drive were the reason for his success. While he had the drive of ten men, he also stood six foot six, and had excellent motor skills, allowing him to dominate his opponents. Statistically, anyone 6'4 and higher is in the 99th percentile, meaning they are 1 in 100. Within the American population, only about 14.5% of men are 6 feet tall and over, yet in the 90s, we all wanted to be "like Mike."

Participation in sports is a great extracurricular activity as it can build discipline, work ethic, and team cooperation; however, it shouldn't take priority over learning. I have worked with countless young kings whose life aspirations are to become professional athletes. I would often ask them what intrigues them the most about being a professional athlete. They would most often respond by saying the money and the fame. When asked to identify which is the most important, they would almost always say the money. This response shows money as being the primary motivator.

Many young kings are so blinded by the media and peers that they cannot imagine themselves becoming wealthy by pursuing an occupation other than sports or entertainment. The media does a great job of celebrating the entertainer's accomplishments; however, they seldom acknowledge black business owners or professionals who have made millions and created thousands of jobs.

Right now, I challenge you to name five African American multi-millionaires who haven't gained their wealth through sports and entertainment. I am sure this would be a challenge, as it was for me. Now, in contrast, I challenge you to name five White American multi-millionaires who have not earned their wealth in sports and entertainment. I'm sure it will be an easier task. These trends and influences often lead to young kings' inability to see themselves as being successful outside of sports and entertainment.

Because of a lack of guidance, many young kings waste precious time chasing hoop dreams and later select low-performing occupations as a default. This happens once they have wasted precious time and will now have to explore other occupations as a default based upon them not being able to do what they wanted to do. Instead of asking our young kings what they want to be when they grow up, I believe we should ask them what they want out of life and assist them in exploring realistic occupations according to their strengths.

As a man, I have discovered being successful has little to do with what you want to do and more to do with what you must do to reach your goals. Young kings should be taught the value of sacrifice and delayed gratification so they may do those things that will bring them rewards in the future. This will require that you develop an individualized plan that will serve as a guide.

This plan should be realistic, measurable, and developed according to the young king's strengths. Once you notice a gift or a strength, begin to cultivate and encourage it. For example, as a child, I didn't perform well academically and had major deficits in math. However, I always had compassion for others. My mother identified my emotional intelligence as a strength and encouraged me to become a helping professional.

Many people tell children, "You can do anything that you put your mind to." While it sounds good, the truth of the matter is that everyone can't do everything. Some people were born with extraordinary gifts and were fortunate to develop them. Every child has a gift; however, because of a lack of observation and support, only a few will ever discover it.

Being able to identify a young king's gift and supporting him in reaching his full potential should be your main objective. This process will allow them to develop a sense of purpose and obligation, which is necessary to cultivate a well-adjusted man. Many parents have a desire for their child to be successful and become well-adjusted; however, they fail at creating a strategic plan. It is commonly known that those who fail to plan, plan to fail. A person without a plan is like a ship without a sail. Plans serve as a blueprint and guide to keep you on course.

When you look at the most effective ethnic groups in America, such as Nigerians, Jews, and Asians, they are a lot more directive in their parenting styles. Too much freedom of choice is not a good thing. For example, I spoke to an Asian American about his upbringing and what made him decide to become a dentist. He responded that ever since he was a child, his parents told him he was going to be a doctor.

However, he was given the freedom to choose his specialty. He became a dentist and never felt that it would be hard because he had been prepared for it. He went further to expand on the study habits and the discipline that was taught in his home. A healthy parenting style should be moderately rigorous and leave less to chance and more to preparation and planning. It is important to explore realistic occupations that will allow young kings to use their gifts and become productive.

Career Aspirations & Economic Security

One of the biggest challenges a young king will encounter in his life is being able to become economically secure and take care of his family. Racial discrimination at its core limits individuals from being able to escape poverty and provide resources that will improve one's quality of life. Being a man in this world is very conditional. We live in a society in which a man is expected to be the protector and the provider. If a man cannot protect and provide, he will not be respected or even acknowledged as being a man.

This is a reality that has caused many young kings to crumble under the pressures of this world or turn to alternate coping mechanisms such as drugs, alcohol, or sex as an escape or form of self-medication. These kinds of coping mechanisms act as barriers that deter them from being able to supply societal demands and expectations, not because of racial discrimination, but because they do not have a plan and are not properly guided.

For this reason, it is imperative that manhood training and development be directive with clear objectives that will not only empower him mentally, but moreover economically. Every young king in training should have a realistic vocational aspiration so that he will be productive. This doesn't mean they cannot explore other interests and dreams; however, it means they must have a way to satisfy their basic psychological needs. There is no place in this world for an unproductive man. It is commonly known that a man that cannot provide for himself adequately will probably turn to criminality and catch pure hell on this earth by experiencing powerlessness, depression, and a lack of resources.

Even if you are not sure of your child's strengths going into his adolescent stages, there are career and personality inventories such as the Myers-Briggs and the Self-Directive Search that can assist in the discovery of strengths and realistic occupations. These assessment tools can identify a person's strengths and provide a realistic occupation that fits along with their personality type. This provides information that can assist you in guiding and directing his path.

Parenting a male of African descent requires you to face all the dangers and obstacles that come along head-on and be prepared to counter each assault with a solution. Being a directive parent comes with great controversy because children are often allowed to do what they want and forced to figure things out on their own. This approach is troubling because there are so many distractions and alternative forms of negative programming that can influence your child's personality and decision-making, including television, social media, music, and negative peers, to name a few. Also, a male's brain is not fully developed until around 25 years old. However, his most formative years are often wasted wandering through life without a genuine sense of purpose.

It is important to create a mission statement for young kings so that they will stay on course. This mission statement should include his obligation to himself, family, and community, which will cause the male to become less self-centered and understand that life is not always about doing what he wants to do. In fact, manhood is about making ultimate sacrifices and doing a lot of things that you don't want to do to secure yourself and your family.

I remember having a deep discussion with an elder, and he made a profound statement. He told me, "As a man, you gotta slinky life." I laughed and thought he was being silly. I then asked him if he was talking about the toy that looked like a coil. He laughed and explained, "Yes, each generation is obligated to gain momentum and advance the next generation further along." I visualized the slinky toy falling end over end and moving off its own momentum with the front part pulling the back part forward. This analogy was branded in my psyche and serves as a reminder of what I must do as a man. For those of you that don't know what a slinky is, Google it!

Young kings should be assisted in exploring realistic goals such as building a business, becoming a professional, or mastering a trade. These three areas will allow the young king to gain not only economic independence but the ability to create their own economy. Nowadays, only the most elite and talented kings can find good jobs. Even if they do, they often must work twice as hard and receive half of the pay in pressured environments.

Throughout my years of counseling men of African descent, many of them have expressed tremendous difficulty trying to assimilate into a corporate culture that required them to play a game that often robs them of their identity. W.E.B. Du Bois said it best by introducing the concept of double consciousness. Du Bois described double consciousness as the struggle African Americans face to remain true to Black culture while conforming to a dominant White society.

Upon reflection, I have noticed significant changes in the racial climate since the office of Presidents Barack Obama and Donald Trump. Since their presidencies, racism has become a lot more overt, especially within the workplace. There are no more policies that ensure that Black men get a seat at the table. Economic discrimination that limit Black men's earning potential place them in a position of powerlessness because they are depending upon those who oppress them to feed them and their families. The time has come to take action and prepare young kings so they will not only survive but thrive.

Relationship

B uilding an intimate relationship with the young king is one of the most important things that is needed to nurture and guide them through life, especially during adolescence. To be clear, adolescent ages are considered 12-21. According to Erik Erikson's psychosocial stages of development, the adolescent stage is commonly referred to as identity vs. role confusion. This is a very challenging time because the young king is experiencing an identity crisis while he is trying to figure out where he fits into the world.

Preparing For Puberty

During this stage, adults and authority figures are even more foreign to their world and their testosterone levels increase 30-fold. For those of you who are unaware, testosterone is the primary sex hormone and is also an anabolic steroid. Anabolic steroids stimulate muscle and tissue growth and cause them to take on a masculine bulky appearance. It also affects mood, temperament, and behaviors. Because of all the biochemical changes the young king experiences as he goes through puberty, we should expect certain challenges and trials that will test you on every level emotionally, physically, and spiritually.

17

At this point in their young lives, adolescents seek to separate themselves from adults and develop their individual selves under the heavy influence of peers. As one can imagine, this is a very dangerous stage because you have the blind leading the blind. This stage of development is very dynamic and requires more support because they are more likely to experiment with sex, negative peer groups, drugs, and alcohol.

Because of all the negative forces working against them, do everything in your power not to miss a day of open communication with them. You must actively have those conversations to find out what is going on in their world. I can't emphasize enough how important it is to "stay in their ear," so that you may be aware of the dynamics that affect their perception. Remember, our young kings are vulnerable during the adolescent stage, and they will need our positive input to push them in the right direction. Having open communication will assist them in gaining clarity through their trials and life experiences with parental guidance.

This level of parental engagement will require that you grow with them and learn a little about everything so that you will be knowledgeable about "the flavor of the day." It is important that we listen to their music, know their peers, understand the current trends, and continuously cultivate the parent/child relationship. Many parents are taken by surprise when they find out their child is involved in something or someone that could have a negative effect on them. If you're active in your child's life, you limit the chances of this happening to you.

No one should have a better relationship with your child than you. So many times, we hear about incidents in which people lose their young kings to the streets because the influences on the outside are greater than the ones on the inside. Therefore, you must cultivate a strong relationship at the early stages of development, so that you can weather the storms that are sure to rise.

Stay Engaged No Matter What

Even if the young king is experiencing a challenge as simple as a peer calling him names, you must be emotionally available to help them process that experience so they can navigate through it. What may be small to you can be catastrophic to them in their world now and in the future. It's not enough to ask, "How was your day?" because you will probably get a response of "good" or "fine." To build a strong parent-child relationship, ask open-ended questions such as, "Has anything interesting happened today?" or "What was the best or worst part of your day?"

Starting the conversation is the toughest part when trying to converse with an adolescent and will require you to be consistent. One way to open the lines of communication is to encourage them to ask you two questions. This exercise forces them to think and provides an opportunity for them to be on the offense instead of always being on defense and having to respond.

For example, one evening I was riding home with my then 16-year-old son after a game, and I asked him if anything interesting happened today. He responded, "No, not really." I probed a little more with no success. I then informed him I would not leave him alone until he asked at least two questions. He took a moment and posed a question that really made me think.

He asked, "What advice would your older self-give your younger self about life, and what makes you happy?"

To the first question, I responded by saying that I would tell my younger self to focus on being your best, be patient, and seek wise counsel. The second question took me a while to answer, and I asked him to give me a moment to process what makes me happy. Later that evening, I answered him by stating, "I am most happy when my family is happy, and I'm able to provide for them." I went further by explaining, "I don't think there is any joy greater than that of a man being able to take care of his family."

This was a powerful moment because I could share information I had never really thought about. It was something that I had no problem sharing, but never would have thought he would be interested in knowing. This exchange not only empowered him but also strengthened our relationship. It opened the door to other conversations regarding what makes him happy, and he could share his aspirations of having a family as well.

Exploring Emotional Awareness

Another technique that is useful in building relationships is the exploration of emotional awareness. For example, I ask young kings on a scale of 1-10—with 1 being the lowest and 10 being the highest—to provide a numerical value of how they are feeling. If they report a low numerical value, such as a 1-5, it provides an opportunity to explore and address any issues at hand. If there is a high numerical value, it provides an opportunity to share and explore. The technique teaches them to do a self-analysis and become aware of their emotions. It also forces a dialog in which you can gather information, build rapport, and develop communication skills.

Throughout my twenty-six years of working with children and families in the helping profession, I have discovered that there are many barriers that hinder a parent from achieving a desirable goal. As caregivers of young kings, we often sound like a broken record, chanting the same things without trying other techniques or approaches. Despite the feelings of frustration and fatigue, it is important that you explore other tactics and reinforce positive values that will serve them in the future.

Even when you don't think they are listening, they are. One of my most rewarding moments as a parent was when my oldest son completed basic training. He told me how much he appreciated my support and me being hard on him. He also informed me if it wasn't for my lectures, support, and riding him, that he would have probably been in jail or dead. This was an affirmation I had long prayed for despite all the challenges we shared. It was confirmation that if we weather the storms, stay engaged, and keep the faith, our labor of love will not go unrewarded. It was at this moment I knew he was becoming a man and could understand my purpose in his life. While I was not his favorite person, I was his greatest resource.

Trust is key because one cannot forge a strong relationship without trust. In the counseling profession, we call it unconditional positive regard. This is when you allow someone to express themselves without fear or judgment. Parents and caregivers should refrain from shaming and blaming so that they can remain objective-driven in their response to the situation at hand. Shaming and blaming the young king will only make them angry and resentful. Feelings of resentfulness are often influenced not by what you say, but how you say it.

The Sandwich Technique

I coach many parents to implement the sandwich technique by offering redirection and correction. The sandwich technique involves identifying a positive attribute first, followed by the negative behavior, which is the target behavior, and concluding with redirection on a positive note. This process not only gives you a chance to address the problem at hand, but it also provides positive reinforcement which will enhance the parent-child relationship. Being harsh in correction is like performing surgery without providing anesthesia and stitching the womb.

The sandwich technique enhances the parent-child relationship and gives you time to develop a strategy to address the issue at hand. I have worked with many families whose children have lost hope and feel that they are alone in the world due to parents being too harsh and critical. This is one reason depression and adolescent suicide are on the rise.

According to the Centers for Disease Control (2020), 18.8% of high school students reported having seriously considered suicide in the past years. It is of great importance that your child knows that no matter what they experience in life, you will never give up or abandon them. This neutralizes a lot of shame and fear, which leads to isolation. I have counseled hundreds of adolescents who believed their parents would stop loving them or inflict bodily harm if they knew what they had done. As caregivers, it is of great importance that they understand they are loved and will be supported no matter what.

I often encourage parents to remember when they did things as a child that made little sense. This kind of reflection helps them to personalize the experience and remain objective-driven in addressing a matter. Remember that I mentioned earlier that their brains won't reach physical maturity until around 25 years old.

Once we separate the emotions from the experience, our logical mind can then make all things a teachable moment. Don't be afraid to make mistakes and remember, there is no such thing as a perfect parent or a perfect child. Building and maintaining a strong parent-child relationship requires patience, time, trust, knowledge, and faith. While we can't guarantee our children will not make mistakes—some of which may break your heart—we must remain steadfast with love and support to see them through.

Separating Emotion From Parenting

Separating your emotions from parenting is one of the most difficult things to do as the parent of a male of African descent. All emotions are not bad; however, being overly emotional impairs a caregiver's ability to make sound decisions in matters concerning their children. This is a big problem because we all know that when we make an emotional decision, it is often a bad one.

Having to raise a young king in a country that has historically lynched, killed, and tortured other young kings simply because of the color of their skin can be paralyzing. Every caregiver of a young king must face the reality that racism is real and being a male of African descent is like caring for a child that has a target on their back. Through years of experience, I have found that caregivers of males of African descent often try to cram as much information into them as possible, knowing they must live in a world in which they will encounter discrimination and hate that could cost them their lives. This cruel reality causes caregivers of young kings to parent out of fear.

If you don't have a certain level of fear while trying to raise a male of African descent in America, I would say that you would be delusional or disconnected from reality. The names of men of African descent who have been slain by a system of white supremacy—most Honorable Martin Luther King, Emmett Till, Trayvon Martin, Tamir Rice, and George Floyd, just to name a few—serve as a testament and gives us the right to be terrified. Throughout American history, the descendants of Africans who were enslaved suffered many blows through 246 years of chattel slavery, 100 years of Jim Crow laws, 34 years of redlining, the overrepresentation of Black men in the Vietnam War, and mass incarceration laws.

The greatest atrocity committed against people of color is not slavery, but the trauma experienced through years of systematic torture and discrimination. There has never been any type of reparations or treatment to address the residual effects of the cruel and inhumane treatment of our people. The trauma of being treated as less than, brutalized, and bred and sold as livestock is a crime against God and humanity.

Sadly, it is something that has never been remedied or addressed. Many people claim these events happened 400 years ago and have no influence on people today. However, recent scientific studies of Epigenetics have provided evidence that trauma leaves a chemical marker on a person's genes and is passed down to subsequent generations. This means the trauma a mother experiences passes through her womb to the child and so forth. Trauma has a negative effect on the areas of the brain that affect memory and impulse control, which causes strong emotional reactivity.

Most times, slavery has affected the way people of African descent raise their children. Dr. Joy DeGruy Leary, renowned for coining the term *post-traumatic slave syndrome*, researched the residual effects of trauma experienced by the descendants of Africans that were enslaved. In her book titled *Post Traumatic Slave Syndrome*, she researched the effects of multigenerational trauma resulting from centuries of slavery and institutionalized racism. She shed light on the dehumanization and trauma experienced by those who were enslaved, as well as their offspring. Dehumanization is depriving a person of their humanity and treating them like animals. This allowed benefactors of slavery to escape cognitive dissonance or moral consequence. To justify years of enslavement, torture, and murder, European nations convinced themselves that people of African descent were animals or savages. Our very survival is a testament to our resilience and greatness.

Fear-based parenting causes the brain to be flooded with adrenaline and stress hormones. Those stress hormones make it difficult to think critically, affecting decision-making. It also causes caregivers to resort to excessive corporal punishment and intimidation. Throughout my years of experience, fear-based parenting has been a common theme, especially among African Americans. This is not a recent phenomenon, as African American parenting methods have traditionally been fear-based. Many scholars suggest fear-based parenting and overutilization of corporal punishment are remnants of slavery. Africans who were enslaved had to punish their young kings severely so that they would learn lessons to escape the slave master's wrath.

I can recall many parents expressing their frustrations in family therapy, saying, "I just as well beat him because if the White man gets hold of him, he will kill him." This had been a saying that I heard as a child as well. The intent was not to hurt the child. Instead, it was an attempt to correct them before they would be subjected to a person who didn't have their best interest in mind. Someone who was keener on overall punishment than making the incident a learning experience. Fear-based parenting has been passed down for generations and has influenced many caregivers in raising males of African descent. This trend passes from one generation to the next because people often parent the way they have been parented. The consequence of being motivated by fear often causes caregivers to become overemotional, too strict, or too indulgent in their parenting methods. This often leads to young kings becoming overly emotional, passive, or overly aggressive.

Physiologically, whenever people are overwhelmed by emotions or stress, information cannot be processed through their prefrontal cortex. The prefrontal cortex is the part of the brain responsible for reasoning and problem-solving. When responding to stress, the brain is flooded with adrenaline and cortisol, which triggers the fight or flight response. When the fight or flight response is triggered by the caregiver, they don't have the option to run, so they use corporal punishment to remedy the situation.

I am not opposed to the use of corporal punishment; however, it is often overused as opposed to taking a cognitive approach to parenting. Excessive corporal punishment inflicts pain and intimidation, which teaches the young king how to be fearful or fearless instead of using critical thinking skills to solve problems and learn lessons. The cognitive approach to parenting takes time and, historically, caregivers of young kings have not had that luxury.

As a father, I must admit my biggest challenge has been separating my emotions from parenting. As parents or caregivers, we are often influenced by fear or the worst-case scenario. We often exaggerate the negative instead of trying to find the positive and make it a teachable moment. I can recall an incident that occurred with my oldest son. He was 11 years old and had been selected to go on a field trip to Washington D.C. with his school.

To prepare for his departure, I gave him more than enough money. Aside from that, I took $20 and placed it in his shoe under the cushion so that it would be used in case of an emergency. I then had a detailed conversation with him regarding keeping the emergency money until he got home and acting as if he didn't have it. The trip only lasted for two days. On the second day, I received a call from his teacher informing me he did not have money to eat, and boy was I heated. I couldn't wait until he got home so that I could address the matter.

I was "38 hot" and had so many emotions running through my mind—shame, frustration, anger, and disappointment, to name a few. That evening, I drove to the school to pick him up and was waiting with all the other parents in the pickup line. As soon as he got in the car, I started yelling at him about not following instructions and how he made his family look bad. I looked into his eyes, and he had fear in them. I stopped mid-sentence and asked him, "Son, how do you feel?"

He responded, "Mad." I paused for a moment, took some deep breaths, and realized it was not my intention to make him mad. After gaining control of my emotions, I realized I was projecting my toxic feelings onto him. His demeanor changed as he began to cry. I had to remind myself, just as I told many parents, that his brain is not fully developed yet. By allowing my emotions to get the best of me, I was not being effective. This made me check myself and realize how wrong I was. As I fell into an emotional state, it only made him angry. I apologized to him for losing my temper and explained my feelings of disappointment and shame because it made me look as if I didn't provide for him.

I had to ask myself, *how can I teach him a lesson so that he learns to be more responsible?* I decided to sleep on it, and the next morning while taking him to school, I heard a payday loan commercial on the radio. I had an epiphany and realized how I could, as my mother would say, "fix him." Whenever he got home from school, I asked him for his piggy bank in which he had about $60. His eyes stretched wide as he brought the piggy bank into the living room.

I asked him how much money he borrowed from the teacher; he informed me it was $10. I then gave him a lesson in borrowing money and educated him about interest rates. I instructed him to write a letter of apology to his teacher with a repayment of the $10, along with $5 interest awarded to me for my pain and suffering. This consequence, along with extra chores, got his attention, and taught him a lesson he still remembers to this very day.

I was able to correct the negative and turn it into a positive. When parenting a young king, we should take a similar approach when the child's offense is not life-threatening. All consequences must be fair, firm, and consistent to change behaviors and teach positive values that can be applied throughout their lives. It is understandable that many parents simply don't have the tools to deal with the trials and undesirable behaviors, which typically lead to feelings of anger and frustration. Let's discuss this for a moment.

Anger is a secondary emotion that typically only surfaces after there are feelings of fear, shame, or hurt. Instead of being able to process these emotional responses, it often causes parents to use tactics such as intimidation, verbal abuse, and excessive spanking. Whenever a parent approaches a situation with heavy emotional undertones, they often transfer them onto the child. This process has a negative effect on the child and causes him to shut down or become fearful. Be careful to use active listening and allow him to express his thoughts without immediately redirecting or correcting them. For example, caregivers often try to correct or redirect before they have even heard the whole story. This causes a caregiver to miss out on gathering information that could expand their understanding of what the young king is experiencing.

Parenting methods should be objective driven. The main priority should be to teach a lesson that will equip the young king in making sound decisions in the future. Many times, we miss the opportunity to teach because of our own emotional frustrations or simply not being aware of the child's needs. As a therapist, I teach parents how to view the world from their child's perspective, so that I can provide clarity on the issue that is at hand. Many parents are quick to judge and punish instead of trying to understand what the child's needs were at that moment. I have had countless parents come to therapy because their child is acting out in school without understanding the root cause of their behaviors.

Some of the biggest complaints parents have about young kings between the ages of eight and twelve, are showing off in class, impulsiveness, being aggressive, and following the wrong crowd. Showing off typically occurs out of a need to be seen or validated. Impulsivity is often a reaction to a lack of structure or discipline in the home. Aggression is often a fear-based behavior that occurs out of a need to be protected or empowered.

Following the wrong crowd is often an expressed need to belong or be accepted. These are all environmental factors that have nothing to do with a chemical imbalance and are often misdiagnosed as Attention Deficit Hyperactive Disorder (ADHD). Many medical professionals have been guilty of treating these symptoms with psychotropic medications instead of getting to the root cause of these behaviors.

Out of all the young kings I have evaluated that have been previously diagnosed with ADHD, only about 20% of them were valid. Many of their symptoms were influenced by environmental factors, and the medical professionals were simply not culturally competent or thorough in their evaluation. Cultural sensitivity is necessary because it plays an important role in how diverse populations express themselves, cope with stress, and seek help. For example, a White male therapist may not understand some customs, norms, and behaviors of the Black family system. This places the practitioner at a disadvantage, and he may not build rapport or under-stand the information gathered during the assessment process. This lack of understanding often leads to misdiagnoses and children being prescribed drugs that have a long-term effect on their brain development.

I have examined countless young kings who have been diagnosed with ADHD as early as age 4 by a pediatrician. I can recall evaluating a 5-year-old male of African descent that had been previously diagnosed with ADHD. After conducting a thorough evaluation, it was revealed that his mother was homeless and in a domestic violence situation in which she was being physically abused in the child's presence. The caregiver was not able to provide a structured environment in the home because she was in survival mode. The medical practitioner was not aware of these dynamics and was not trained to explore the issues that directly impact a child's behavioral symptoms. The pediatrician did not see the old scars on the mother's face or the pain in her eyes during the child's evaluation. Essentially, the practitioner treated the child without consideration of the mother or the environmental factors.

This is an atrocity because, again, many children have been prescribed stimulants that have long-term effects on their brain development. I have seen many young kings transition from attention deficit disorder to op-positional defiant disorder. From oppositional defiant disorder to mood disorder. From mood disorder to bipolar disorder and depression. The train doesn't end there because many of the young kings that were misdi-agnosed often find themselves in the criminal justice system, which further perpetuates a systematic issue.

I do not oppose the treatment of ADHD; however, caregivers should educate themselves about the diagnosis and seek culturally sensitive practitioners to rule out any environmental factors that influence behavioral symptoms. As a child, I easily could have been diagnosed as having ADHD; however, the diagnosis just emerged in the 1980s. I often fidgeted, was impulsive, daydreamed, and performed poorly academically.

As I reflect upon my early childhood, I was born in September, so I was enrolled in an elementary school with children who were a year older than me. One year is not long for adults; however, it was tremendous from a developmental perspective. As a child, being in a class with children having a one-year developmental advantage caused a great deal of anxiety and stress. Children who are placed in pressured environments often display symptoms of ADHD not because they have a chemical imbalance, but because they are simply trying to cope and adjust. There are so many variables that should be explored and ruled out before a diagnosis is rendered.

Please understand this information is not meant to discredit any helping professionals; however, I hope to encourage parents to do their due diligence in making sure their child is treated as a unique individual. Cookie-cutter treatment is a parent's worst enemy because everyone is different and should be treated as such. Many behavioral health programs are treating adolescents with medications first because of a lack of resources or clinicians to provide individualized care. Caregivers should explore second opinions and try alternative methods of treating behavioral symptoms as opposed to relying upon medications.

Parenting is a job that requires 24-hour/365 days of work, sacrifice, and focus to succeed. There are no days off. Even when you are sick, tired, fed up, and frustrated, you must persevere and make the best decision to meet the child's needs. Often, we get frustrated with some of the things naturally occurring in a child's development. We need to understand that every child is different. They are trying to learn, and cope with life's challenges. We should expect them to make mistakes and provide redirection and instruction.

It should be your aim to prepare your child for every experience before it happens. Much effort should be devoted towards the development of critical thinking skills and problem-solving. This will allow them to discover their greatest ability, which is being able to think rationally, and problem-solve. As caregivers, we must always strive to separate our emotions from our parenting because the young king is learning how to manage his emotions from his interactions with you. Whenever you become emotional during a conflict, they are taught and socialized to respond without restraint or self-control.

Police Etiquette

Nowadays, we are forced to face a harsh reality that every officer of the peace does not come in peace. America has had a front-row seat in watching many lynchings and slayings of unarmed males of African descent at the hands of bad police. This is a crisis that we must prepare our young kings for as we know they will encounter racial bias, especially from law enforcement. The sad part about police brutality is it has been going on since the beginning of American history to oppress and terrorize the descendants of Africans who had been released from the plantations. The very origins of policing can be traced back to slave patrols responsible for capturing runaway slaves and returning them to their masters.

Many parents are doing the best they can to raise our young kings; however, they often become overly emotional in their interventions and model how he should conduct himself in a crisis. Young kings must be taught how to manage their emotions even in the absence of a strong male figure in the home. Those young kings who are not taught to manage their feelings are more temperamental and make emotional decisions because they have not been trained to handle authority.

This is critical because society may tolerate a woman becoming emotional; however, being overly emotional as a man may jeopardize his life, especially when encountering the police. I often have serious conversations with young kings about being cool under pressure. We see our young kings as being boys, but police officers see a Black male with the potential to take their lives. Therefore, we must take time to train young kings in pressured therapeutic environments to get them ready for the world.

As an adolescent male of African descent raised in the south, I have tasted the bitter reality of being treated unfairly by the police. To this day, seeing flashing blue lights causes an immediate stress response in my body that can only be described by one word: terror. As a helping professional, I realized this is a problem that must be addressed by training our young kings to survive encounters with bad police officers. Proper training will teach them how to neutralize a situation that could be fatal.

In my practice, I train young kings in police etiquette to prepare them for real-life encounters during traffic stops. Within my police etiquette training model, there are several areas that must be addressed.

Traffic Stop Simulation

Remain calm and present a non-offensive posture. This means hands on the steering wheel, positioned at 9&3 when being engaged by law enforcement.

Remain calm and take deep breaths.

Request permission to present readily accessible identification and proper credentials if driving.

Remain calm and compliant, even if the law enforcement officer is on edge.

Request permission to call the parent of the caregiver.

Remain calm even if you are denied permission to call.

Do not resist arrest and allow the officer to arrest you peacefully.

Within my program, I simulate by using role play with young kings to create a scenario in which they will not only be tested but instigated to cause an emotional response as a trigger. As people of color, we view things from a moralistic perspective without understanding all the dynamics that are at work. For example, many police shootings are committed by law enforcement officers who are not only prejudiced but also are fearful of Black men.

This puts them in a fight or flight response in which they are on edge and not able to think clearly. Fear often cripples individuals from being rational. Within my course, I provide an example of how the use of police etiquette techniques has assisted me by avoiding a calamity.

I was traveling to Atlanta on Interstate 20 and was pulled over by a White law enforcement officer while going 65 mph in a 70-mph speed zone around 2:00 p.m. The police officer was headed east in the opposite lane and cut through the median. The moment I saw the blue lights, my adrenaline raged. Even though I knew I was not speeding, I was nervous and scared. Because of the luxury vehicle I was driving, I instantly knew I was being profiled when we saw each other through the windshield.

I pulled over to the shoulder of the highway and clutched the steering wheel with two hands and sat motionless. The cop came up to my window clutching his gun with his right hand in an offensive position and shouted through the window, "You know why I stopped you, right?"

"No sir," I responded.

He said, "You have an illegal tint on your windows."

"No sir, the car has a factory tint from the manufacturer."

"What did I say?" He snapped and continued with an attitude, "Where are you going?"

At that moment, I felt disrespected and thought, *"None of your damn business."* However, I knew that would escalate the incident.

I responded, "Sir, I am going to pick my daughter up for spring break from Atlanta."

Sighing heavily, he then asked for my driver's license and registration.

"Sir, may I reach in the glove box with my right hand to obtain it?" I asked.

He said yes, so I took my right hand from the steering wheel and handed him my credentials. After checking my tags and registration, he said, "I'm gonna give you a warning this time." He walked back to his patrol car and sped off.

This incident could have gone wrong in so many ways. The sad thing about it is that I had to be calm and submissive because it could have cost me my life. I later made a formal complaint about the incident so that it may be addressed administratively. As caregivers, we should take our young kings through role plays and simulations of friendly and hostile traffic stops to test their ability to react to prevent conflict. This intervention is much needed and will equip them with the tools needed to survive.

We must train our young kings when encountering law enforcement officers to be as wise as a serpent, yet as gentle as a dove. I always tell my sons to submit to law enforcement, even if it means they must swallow their pride or face wrongful arrest. The most important thing is that they make it home safe and sound. This doesn't mean the matter will not be addressed legally; however, it ensures they will live to see another day.

Sensitive Topics

Young kings should be encouraged to discuss sensitive topics with caregivers, even if it makes both parties feel uncomfortable. When discussing sensitive topics with young kings, I imagine myself grabbing a charging bull by the horns. This image helps me to face my fears and address the incident at hand. If you don't take the matter seriously and address it, there is a strong possibility that it will eventually hurt you, the child, and others. The reason I mentioned hurting you first is that throughout my experiences as a counselor, parents would much rather be in trouble than their child. There is no pain greater than seeing your child suffer and not being able to help them. As parents or caregivers, we would much rather carry that cross for them.

There are so many issues adolescents experience that could have been prevented or avoided if we addressed those sensitive topics on the front end. The more uncomfortable the topic addressed in the past, the easier it gets to discuss sensitive matters in the future. This allows them to share experiences without fear and shame. Real-life experiences can be used as examples that will teach lessons and strengthen relationships. It is important that the young king trusts in you and understands your role as their protector and guide.

This is a significant challenge because adolescents often believe that adults are out of touch and do not know how things are at that moment. Therefore, you should continuously share information and insight that is relevant in the past, present, and future. Caregivers often miss opportunities to discuss sensitive topics that can provide clarity and be a catalyst for learning.

For example, I have had many caregivers in family therapy sessions report catching their young kings watching pornography or masturbating. Under these circumstances, the caregiver often makes the mistake of being punitive or making them feel bad or ashamed. Instead of punishing them, it can be treated as an opportunity to have an open discussion about sex and their perception of sexuality. This kind of discussion will give you an opportunity to educate them about the harmful effects that pornography has on the mind and interpersonal relationships. Also, it will provide an opportunity to probe so that you may learn how long they have been consuming porn to determine whether it is experimental or habitual. This process will equip you with the information needed to formulate a plan for censorship or interventions needed.

During the adolescent stages, a young king's world seems to have nothing in common with their parents or other adults. During this phase, you must be committed to sharing as much useful information from the past as possible so that they can identify the similarity in experiences. Identifying similarities in experience to build rapport can be achieved by caregivers, no matter their age or gender. I often hear single mothers say they can't reach their young king; however, they have had many experiences that he may learn from. An appropriate amount of self-disclosure can strengthen the parent-child relationship and cause the young king to see their caregiver as being "real." This doesn't mean that you should air all your dirty laundry; however, attachment and relationships are strengthened through sharing.

For example, share an incident in which you were a poor judge of character within an interpersonal relationship. This gives you an opportunity to share some of your beliefs and perceptions that were changed because of your experiences. It has been my experience that everybody has played the fool at least one time. Within a few moments, you'd have an opportunity to share life experiences and teach valuable lessons.

Accepting No Wooden Nickels

When raising young kings, there are issues that often go unaddressed because the caregiver allows the child to escape responsibility for his actions. As a young king around 8 years old, I remember living in a housing complex where there were several abandoned units. I was very mischievous as a child and picked up a rock and wanted to break a window so badly. I remember an intense desire to throw the rock and see the glass shatter, just as other children had done in the neighborhood. The only thing that stopped me was knowing the consequence was going to be serious. Had I believed there was a 10% chance I could get away with it, I would have broken the window. Because my parents were so engaged and had held me accountable in the past, I decided not to break it.

Children are master manipulators and are skillful in escaping responsibility for their actions, even if it requires trying to make their caregivers seem as if they are the problem. I can't tell you how many times I have doubted my decision-making in parenting my young kings based on them "giving me a wooden nickel." The wooden nickel was a wooden coin placed in circulation during the Great Depression because of coin short-ages. After the depression ended, the wooden nickel became useless and a symbol of scarcity. So, whenever a child tries to give an excuse and escape consequences for their actions, I refer to it as a wooden nickel.

Sometimes my children told a story that was so believable, it forced me to launch a thorough investigation, only to reveal they were lying and trying to escape consequences for their actions. Many parents consciously and subconsciously allow their young kings to escape responsibility for their actions because they believe in their story and accept the wooden nickel.

As a result, caregivers often become emotional and resort to yelling, threatening, and procrastination, which almost never works. Often, par-ents procrastinate and ignore signs or symptoms that show there is a prob-lem. Procrastination is a waste of time and often lets things fester like a sore, as opposed to addressing it immediately with proper interventions. Like a sore, if issues are not immediately addressed, it often leads to more damage.

Whenever a parent allows a child to escape responsibility for their ac-tions, they are rewarding negative behaviors. For example, if a young king gets in trouble in school for class disruption, the excuse would often be, "Someone was picking on me," "It wasn't me," or "The teacher doesn't like me." If the young king can escape the consequence of disrupting class, he has learned that he can get out of trouble by lying. This causes the young king to become more skillful in lying and manipulation.

Now, a problem that was as simple as classroom disruption has rein-forced undesirable behaviors. If these types of behaviors and perceptions are not addressed, they can cause the development of criminal thought patterns that can lead to criminal behaviors. I encourage caregivers to launch a full investigation and act as a judge when addressing undesirable behaviors. A judge must be able to assess all the evidence without emotion and bias. This will allow the caregiver to hold them accountable to maintain order and teach lessons in life. Because you are holding them accountable, you can expect that you will not be their favorite person. While the relationship is critical in a parent-child relationship, friendship is not. To be clear, you are not their friend, nor should you expect to be liked or loved when holding them accountable. It is most important that they respect you and understand your role and expectations within the parent/child relationship. You have a job to do and must remain objective-driven to achieve the goals that have been previously established.

As an engaged parent, you will encounter many trials and tribulations. However, you must be able to respond and adjust. No one is perfect, and it is because of our imperfections that we must be prepared for anything. It is critical that we know our limitations and be receptive to getting support from culturally sensitive professionals to intervene if necessary.

The Importance of Early Intervention

Early intervention is very critical because it will provide an opportunity to be proactive in a situation versus being reactive. There is an old saying that goes, "Why try and stop a fire that starts in your kitchen when it gets in your bedroom?" In other words, a person should stop a fire as soon as it starts, not once it spreads too rapidly. We often procrastinate and ignore some signs or symptoms that indicate there is a problem. This is a waste of time and often leads to more damage that could have been resolved with a simple remedy.

For example, we now live in a world in which adolescents have access to vape pens and candied edibles laced with high levels of (THC) tetrahydrocannabinol. THC is the chemical compound found in marijuana that artificially spikes dopamine levels in the brain and provides an intense feeling of euphoria we commonly call being "high." Because adolescents' brains are still developing, the consumption of THC has been proven to have a negative effect on their mental health, often leading to addiction, anxiety, depression, and long-lasting mental health disorders.

Because of legalization and new ways of consuming THC, it is easily accessible and does not need to be smoked. Your child can develop a serious addiction over a long period while going unnoticed. As a licensed addictions counselor, I have treated countless adolescents who are chemically dependent, and their parents are totally unaware until a crisis occurs.

Usually, it takes time to build dependence, and it begins in the experimentation phase by taking the first drink or smoke. By staying engaged and observant, you will catch them in the experimentation stage and notice any changes, such as your child acting strangely, having cloudy eyes, and eating excessively. All of which are symptoms of consuming marijuana or drug usage. If you observe these symptoms early, you should have them drug screened immediately and follow up with an evaluation by a mental health professional. This immediate intervention would stop the fire in the kitchen before it gets to the bedroom.

Many caregivers accept wooden nickels throughout the child's life and later realize they have created a monster they can no longer control by not holding them accountable. A young king's mind can easily be contaminated with negative peers, values, environmental factors, and experiences. Cultivating a young king is like maintaining a garden in the spring. While you plant good seeds and water them, you must be mindful that the weeds will always grow faster than the plants. You must be consistent in weeding out those thoughts, beliefs, and behaviors that will cause serious issues.

It is important that you continuously hold the young king accountable so they may understand that for each action, there is a consequence that will follow. Many young kings find themselves in a courtroom trying to escape consequences for some behaviors they have been able to get away with in much of their lives. The criminal justice system will not be as forgiving and traditionally has not been fair in its treatment of males of African descent.

Catch Them Doing Right

We have spent a lot of time discussing the importance of holding young kings accountable; however, it is equally, if not more, important to reward them for positive behaviors. This doesn't mean we have to pay them for doing the right thing. Many times, simple acknowledgment and verbal appreciation will do. Positive reinforcement is the most effective way to change and improve human behaviors. Unfortunately, we have been programmed to always see the negative behaviors and ignore the positive ones. This is an issue that often causes young kings to grow weary in well-doing.

I have sat in front of countless parents who recite a long list of all the things their child is doing wrong; however, when asked what they are doing right, there is a pause. As a clinician, I often encourage parents to identify strengths because they are so consumed with the negative symptoms at hand. This is the case with many of us, especially as it relates to our children. This doesn't make us terrible parents; it's simply the way our minds work.

Our brains have been wired to find problems and solutions, not strengths. This is a cruel reality, but it's natural and is more in line with survival skills. For example, if you are living in the wilderness in a cold climate, you will not celebrate how much firewood you cut to survive through the night. After you cut the wood, you would immediately move on to the next task, whether it be gathering food, making a fire, or drawing water. If we really evaluate the situation, I am sure that there is something noteworthy of praise in every child.

Being overly critical often leads to resentment and frustration from the child. Therefore, as parents, we must take time to identify strength in our young kings, even when they are not fulfilling our expectations. Remember, things can always be worse. Even in the darkest hour, we can find a glimmer of hope in all things.

Using wise sayings and creative story telling

U sing parables, metaphors, and wise sayings can be very impactful in cultivating critical thinking skills and teaching important life lessons. My mother and father were Masters of Teaching pearls of wisdom using wise sayings and parables. They consistently used these strategies throughout my life to get my attention when simple communication wouldn't suffice. My mother was from Georgetown, South Carolina.

She was born in a small community called Choppee and raised in Midway. This small community was very similar to an African village in that it was isolated from Whites and had little interaction with other communities. These were small tight-knit communities in which they had strong family values, owned land, and had their own stores. They held onto their African morals and dialect, which is nowadays called Gullah Geechee. The Gullah people are descendants of enslaved Africans from several tribal groups from west and central Africa.

My father was born in the 1930s to a family of sharecroppers in Clarendon County. Sharecropping was a modified version of slavery in the south to keep the descendants of slaves on the farm. The more children they had, the more likely they would be allowed to stay on the land. He was the second to the oldest of nine children, all of which were exploited for free labor for food and poor housing. He nor his siblings could attend school because they were used to work in the fields.

His parents did not own property and much of his lineage was not traceable. Despite being denied a formal education, my father was very intelligent and proud. He couldn't read nor write; however, he had what many people lack today: common sense. Throughout our lives, our parents would tell us stories as opposed to giving us the answers or solutions. These sayings would be prescribed at the right time, when necessary, as if it was medicine. They would be skillfully delivered sometimes with satirical humor to force us to look at things from a more elevated perspective.

They would say things like, *"When's the last time you seen a red bird and a blackbird fly together?"* This simply means that you must choose your friends wisely and class yourself among positive people.

Another one was, *"It ain't behind you, it's in front of you!"* This meant that they had already been through things that you are yet to experience, and it also was a warning not to be stubborn.

My father's favorite was, *"Son, you're wronger than two left shoes."* This meant that no matter how you tried to rationalize it, you are still wrong and can't make it right. Whenever he hit me with that one, I knew I was wrong and would visualize my feet with two left shoes, trying to walk around in public.

Another one was, ***"You shouldn't have to eat the whole hog to know it's pork. Why wait until you get down to the hoof, snout, and hair to know it's pork?"*** This means that if you know something is not good for you, let it go. This was another classic that was prescribed when I was stuck on stupid and wouldn't listen to reason.

My mother, in her Gullah Geechee accent, would say, ***"Go head bump, baby, bump! Bump your a$$ like a bullfrog!"*** I would visualize myself as being a big frog jumping up and down on the sidewalk. With every leap, I would land painfully on my behind. This analogy meant you were being stubborn as well.

My parents would also share adult dilemmas, which men would commonly fall victim to. One of my favorites was, ***"Son, don't put your money in the hairy bank! You can make deposits, but you can't get any withdrawals!"*** This simply meant don't allow women to exploit you for your resources in exchange for sex.

As you can see, I can recall several sayings that were ingrained in me as a child. Using creative storytelling and parables really made sensitive conversations fun. They acknowledged the commonality of the human experience. My brothers and I were able to grasp serious concepts that many of our peers had not even been exposed to. Our peers would often call us old people's children because of our old-fashioned values and perspective on life. Still, the interventions our parents provided made us less susceptible to becoming followers and more comfortable in leadership roles.

These and many other wise sayings have taught me precious lessons that have been instrumental in my growth and development. They are precious pearls of wisdom that I share with my young kings and others in need at the right time. As stated earlier, many times, we as parents or caregivers yell, lecture, or try to use fear tactics to address issues. This usually causes an emotional response, and the young king is robbed of an opportunity to learn. As an adult, we often lose touch with reality, and let me not forget to remind you again of the many foolish things you did as a child.

There's an old saying which says that adults are but grown-up children. This saying usually humbles me and provides perspective in seeking to understand what the young king is thinking in their motivation. As a caregiver, this forces you to look at life through their eyes to make sense of their behaviors. The process also forces more inquiries and often leads to an expansion of parental awareness. There are so many dynamics in life that only are revealed via sharing and open communication.

When the young king is allowed to share some of their trials and experiences without judgment, you can vicariously learn through them and have a better understanding of their reality. Even if their reality makes little sense, explain to them why it made little sense without shaming or blaming. You should do so in a way they can understand. These types of interventions will force them to think and cultivate critical thinking skills.

Throughout my years of practice, I have discovered that most of the problems experienced can be resolved or prevented by providing support and insight. Once you begin to cultivate young kings' critical thinking skills, they will begin to think independently and ask questions that may challenge your awareness. This is great because this shows they are using their cognitive muscles. One of the greatest teachers known within the scriptures used parables to teach life-changing lessons.

Jesus specialized in using parables that forced the audience to use deductive reasoning. Deductive reasoning is a logical process in which a conclusion is based on the similarity of multiple experiences that are assumed to be true. It's also referred to as top-down logic. This kind of top-down logic allows the individual to test a hypothesis with an existing theory.

To clarify my point, people often are not receptive to strong arguments without being able to take part in the learning and discovery process. Asking questions is one of the most successful strategies for getting others involved in the learning process. Even if they do not understand the parable because of a lack of understanding, you have at least been successful in stimulating thought and have planted a seed.

Using parables and wise sayings provides you with an opportunity to not only teach a lesson but also have fun. Wise sayings and parables confirm the reality that what they are experiencing is simply a replay of an event that has occurred many times before.

Creative Storytelling

Creative storytelling is powerful because it makes a lesson more impressionable. To use creative storytelling in teaching a lesson as a caregiver, you must have a plot, theme, characters, action, and a little suspense. This allows you to frame an artificial reality to teach a lesson. My creative storytelling would begin by using the phrase:

The Gospel According to: XXXXXX

The Xs represent a character I wish to be the star of the lesson. Once I shared a few stories using this phrase, the young king would be on alert, just like a faithful member in church awaiting a powerful message. Creative stories should always apply to their situation. They should also have a moral, and it wouldn't hurt to add a little humor. Here's an example below of creating storytelling that acknowledges how sex or lust can influence a person to make a poor decision in life.

Now, without further delay, I would like to share the **Gospel According to Peter Rabbit**: "There once was a rabbit named Peter. Every now and then, he would leave his hole to run across town. On his way, he would look both ways and cross the railroad track to get to his destination. As time went on, he got comfortable with hopping the tracks and became a little less cautious. One day, he hopped on the tracks, thinking that he could beat the train. Once he got over to the other side, he noticed the train had clipped his tail off. The rabbit went back across the track to get it and another train came, ran him over, and killed him. The poor rabbit lost his life over a *little piece of tail*!"

Using creative storytelling will also provide insight and wisdom they can apply when they encounter similar challenges in life. Leave no stone unturned so they can think about all the dynamics involved in the scenario. Sometimes, I give them the gospel according to Terrance (myself), so they can understand that I have made bad decisions in life, and through sharing, I wish they learn from mine.

I often tell young kings that it has taken me over forty-seven revolutions around the sun to learn so many painful lessons, yet I will share so they may be wiser. This will help them avoid the pitfalls and snares that wounded me so they wouldn't have to suffer as I had. It also helps them to understand that life is an ever-evolving experience in which you will have serious challenges. This process allows the young king to look beyond their current circumstance and make adjustments armed with knowledge and wisdom. Could you imagine a 16-year-old king having the knowledge of a 47-year-old? This would place him at a clear advantage.

Throughout life, many elders have taught me valuable lessons and principles through creative storytelling. These creative stories have truly enriched my life in so many ways and provided useful information that aided me in navigating through life. There are certain principles that must be applied in life if you wish to obtain a goal.

Many of the creative stories and wise sayings not only have meaning, but they point you in the direction in which you may find other answers in your own time and way. In the ancient days, scientists were priests and shamans because they had the knowledge and could explain the human experience through storytelling. They used the scientific approach, meaning there are certain ingredients or principles that must be utilized to achieve desired results. If you have any goal, you must be able to sacrifice and apply the principles to succeed.

As elders, we have had many life experiences that can provide wisdom and insight that can foster growth and teach lessons. We should strive to give our young kings the answers to the test. The test is life, and it will continually become more complex with each day, like the stages in a video game. While we can provide many of the answers to the test, we can't take it for them.

Sexuality

Discussing sexuality with young kings has long been a sensitive topic surrounded by taboo because of fear, shame, and a lack of understanding. Sex is one of the strongest natural human desires. It will make a man, or a woman, risk their life and everything they love for a few moments of pleasure. This is commonly known but almost never acknowledged. Throughout history and presently, sex has been at the root of many scandals, betrayals, and even murder. According to Maslow's hierarchy of needs, sex is a basic psychological need.

Within the African American community, it is a topic that has been much neglected. Not discussing sex with a young king is like nature giving him a loaded gun. However, as caregivers, we neglect discussing its proper use or firearm safety. According to a study conducted by the Centers for Disease Control (CDC), nearly half of the pregnancies in the United States were unintended. The data also reports that males of African descent have more unintended pregnancies than Whites and Hispanic males. Many young kings become sexually active before they are mature enough to handle a relationship and make rational decisions.

There are so many negative influences that celebrate and encourage the participation of casual sex and promiscuity, especially in the African American community. Nowadays, many young kings are being contaminated by music and media that not only promote sexual promiscuity but also influence young kings to feel as if their manhood is contingent upon them being sexually irresponsible and reckless.

This is not a new issue; however, it has gotten worse because of exposure to sexually suggestive music and media. I can remember having the same pressures and expectations from peers and older men whose identity and self-worth depended on how many sexual partners they had. This is an issue that must be addressed so that you, as a caregiver, can provide guidance and insight about sex and relationships. I have counseled so many young kings that have been picked on for having their V-card. Having your V-card means you haven't lost your virginity.

Sex has long been an elephant in many rooms, and we no longer have the luxury of ignoring it. Many parents have challenges discussing sexuality with their sons because of their lack of understanding and shame. It's not enough to discuss the biology and physiology of sex without exploring beliefs and perceptions. As parents, we should begin educating our young kings about sex as early as 10 years old so that they will know the changes occurring in their bodies now and in the future. This process will provide them with awareness and trust because it will enable you to explain the physiological changes before, they occur.

Between the ages of 10 and 11, the sex hormone, testosterone increases. Around puberty, testosterone levels increase 30-fold and sex becomes a major area of interest, whether or not you talk to them about it. When you look at things from a biological perspective, males have been designed to seek sexual gratification and are one of the few mammals that can have sex year-round. An adolescent male can produce several million sperm per day at a rate of about 1,500 per second. This biological evolution often causes conflict because the genitals of males mature long before their brains do.

Aside from that, pleasure is coupled with a male's ejaculation, and many scientists believe that this is nature's way of tricking humans into having sex. If reproduction wasn't pleasurable, many humans wouldn't reproduce, causing low birth rates and possible extinction. Sexual energy is also creative energy. If properly harnessed and channeled, it can build civilizations or destroy them. Because of the high testosterone levels, males may have tendencies to become more impulsive, irritable, emotional, and aggressive. It is important to acknowledge the chemical changes within their bodies and keep them engaged in healthy, age-appropriate activities that will teach discipline, work ethic, and self-control. Providing a basic understanding of sex can help them form a healthy perception of sexuality and interpersonal relationships.

Traditionally, young kings have not received guidance during this stage and rely on peers or pornography to educate them about sex. This is one of the biggest reasons young kings are misguided and often become teenage parents or contract sexually transmitted infections.

In America, sex has been monetized and perverted, which has caused people to view it only as a means of pleasure. Pleasure is only a byproduct of sex, which makes the union satisfying and formulates attraction. When discussing sexuality with young kings, I describe sex as a sacred union between two people that might yield offspring. I know this concept sounds old-fashioned; however, if we do not change our perception of sexuality and our relationship with sex, single-parent households, and broken family systems will continually increase.

Sex is also a biological bonding element meant for procreation and to establish long-term attachments. Casual sex causes individuals to develop issues with an attachment that hinders them from forming a connection with a partner. The more a man or woman has casual sex with multiple partners, the less likely they will be satisfied within a monogamous relationship.

There's Nothing "Casual" About Sex

During sexual activity, high levels of oxytocin, which is known as the love or bonding hormone, are released to create a deeper connection. Oxytocin is also released in high volumes when a mother births a child immediately after labor to enhance attachment. The more a person has casual sex, the less oxytocin they will produce, which impairs their ability to form a bond and develop intimate relationships.

Therefore, it is natural to become attached and emotional once humans share their bodies; in street terminology, we call it being "whipped." Being "whipped" or attached to someone after sex is natural and normal. However, in the subculture, only suckers and simps gain attachments after sex. This is a serious issue because males and females were designed to be connected to each other for procreation and to give their offspring an advantage. There are mountains of research and data that reports children raised in intact, two-parent families are healthier, happier, and less likely to suffer from addictions and incarceration. Many young kings have been programmed by a negative subculture to have sex with no kind of emotional connection. It is my professional opinion that sex without connection is a maladaptive coping mechanism. African Americans have experienced a great deal of trauma and shame regarding not being in control of our reproductive rights through slavery and selective breeding.

Many males of African descent use sex as a coping mechanism because it makes them feel good by releasing high levels of dopamine and gives them a false sense of power. Within the negative subculture, hyper-sexuality and promiscuity became a value that was reinforced and esteemed within many communities. This subculture has influenced many young kings to be proud of their ability to gain sexual conquests without connection or responsibility. This is a trap many young kings have fallen into, not because of a lack of morality, but because of a lack of understanding and guidance.

Within the subculture, the peer pressure is so strong that a man is not validated by his peers until he "gets some." It's considered a rite of passage that serves no purpose other than reinforcing values that are counterproductive. Everyone admires the "ladies' man." He is esteemed for having as many sexual conquests as he can obtain. This belief system is still prevalent in our community and often plagues men throughout their adulthood if not addressed.

Nowadays, things have gotten worse because the music and media have infected young queens as well. The industry promotes negative values by influencing them to celebrate promiscuity and sexual irresponsibility. We live in a time in which young queens frequently listen to a genre called "pu$$y rap." Also, I have overheard young queens in the academic environment as young as 12 years old brag about having "WAP." For those who are unaware, "WAP" is synonymous with having wet a$$ pu$$y. Within the subculture, young queens have been reduced to perverse sexual objects. Many popular female rap artists have fallen into the same trap. Instead of promoting murder, they celebrate promiscuity and being vulgar.

This kind of wicked programming influences many young queens' beliefs and perceptions of womanhood. Provocative lyrics in music, along with other issues in the media, directly impact how young kings and queens relate to each other. These kinds of relational dynamics are counterproductive to building strong children and families. We should teach our young kings to be very selective in choosing a mate because the hand that rocks the cradle rules the world. This is an old African proverb that reminds us that our women are the first and most important teachers of the children.

There is much that has been lost that must be rediscovered. The sacred divine mother of all civilizations must awake and take her rightful place if we plan to save our people. I encourage young kings to ask themselves one question before they have sex with a female. Can I trust the woman to raise my child if I died prematurely? This forces the young king to look into the future and think like a man rather than a boy.

We must teach our young kings how to properly court in interpersonal relationships. Many of our young kings are infatuated with romantic love, lust, or physical appearances; all of which are superficial and will often lead to disappointments. Young kings should be taught to seek a partner that is loyal, respectful, supportive, and intelligent. Those are the attributes that are needed to form a strong, long-lasting relationship.

We should encourage our sons to remain celibate until they are mature and responsible enough to handle sexual relationships. Sex is not just a casual act of sharing bodies and seeking pleasure. Sex is also a way of sharing your soul and spirit. This is the kind of wisdom I wished was shared with me as a youth. If we regarded sex as not only a sacred act but also an opportunity to live in the hereafter through our offspring, we would be in a much better state.

Rap Poison

Throughout my years of working with young kings in my counseling practice, one of the biggest culprits that has a negative effect on young kings' personality development is gangster rap. In its origin, gangster rap began as a cry for help from young kings to shed light on the many injustices within impoverished communities of color. The first gangster rappers were telling a story of some of the terrible things that were going on in their lives or neighborhoods.

Something that began as a cry for help influenced a negative subculture. This negative subculture has caused a social illness that is destroying the minds of our young kings. It has become a dominant force in many communities of color and glamorizes being a serial killer, drug dealer, and taking part in any act that will bring economical gain without consideration for the community. As a social scientist and clinician, I am noticing a pattern of pathological behaviors from young kings being influenced by harmful rap lyrics.

Nowadays, about 90% of rap music content is toxic and poisonous. I have worked with hundreds of adolescents over the years that have been psychologically contaminated by what I have defined as *"Rap Poison Syndrome"*.

Some beliefs and perceptions reinforced in toxic rap music are:

Beliefs or perceptions of oneself as being gangster or "hard."

Negative attitude toward interpersonal or sexual relationships.

Negative attitude towards cooperating with police in the event of a crime.

Beliefs or perceptions that criminal behaviors are cool.

Beliefs or perceptions that the usage of illicit drugs is cool.

These are some of the negative perceptions or beliefs that strongly affect the values and decision-making of young kings that are reinforced by toxic rap music. While it has not yet been proven that toxic rap music is the primary cause of these negative symptoms, it is my professional opinion that it has a tremendous influence. The toxic effects of gangster rap are a serious issue and are worthy of further investigation by the scientific community. Many young kings have been so heavily influenced by rap poison they not only display negative behaviors, but they also believe that it is cool.

Our young kings are being programmed to kill each other under a catchy tune or musical hook. There have been 142 murders per 100,000 among young kings in 2021, which is a 74% increase since 2014, according to the *Journal of the American Medical Association* in 2022. Homicide rates are 23 times higher among young kings and nearly four times higher among Hispanic men than White men. While we can't blame toxic rap music for all the homicides, there is a correlation between the two variables. The emergence of gangster rap made it cool and popular to kill a young king with no justification. The engineering of gangster rap serves as a powerful tool in desensitizing and celebrating murder by using terms such as *murk, redrum, popped, bust a cap, wet em' up, 187, leave them stinking* and *"smoking a fool"* as referred to by NWA.

Disclosure, speaking of *"smoking a fool"* which was a term used to describe murder in the movie *Boyz in the Hood*, I recall attending college and crossing the fence to visit some friends at a neighboring university. Those friends were from my hometown, and we were playing cards, consuming alcohol, and watching *Boyz in the Hood* while listening to gangster rap music. As the evening progressed, some of my peers began testing each other by slap boxing and wrestling. I looked around and felt it was a matter of time before someone tried me, so I hopped the fence and went to my dorm room. Later that night, there was a knock on the door around 2:00 a.m. We learned there was a shooting in which my friend had gotten shot at the same gathering I had just left. The sad thing about it, these were not thugs, criminals, nor street people. These were college students that came from good families under the influence of alcohol, toxic media, and rap poison. The victim was shot several times but survived and the offender was incarcerated.

The desensitization of murder is also felt in my hometown in which adolescents refer to murder as murk, hence "Murk City." The harsh reality is when social ills are coupled with self-destructive programming, there is a catastrophic effect. Many of the young kings I serve are truly scared and have experienced so much trauma that many meet full diagnostic criteria for PTSD based on their symptoms. Many males of African descent cannot cope with their harsh realities and react out of a position of fear and pain. When fear and pain is not properly addressed, it often manifests itself as rage and aggression. We see its vicious effects every day when we turn on the news and learn that a Black man has killed someone that speaks like him, dresses like him, and looks like him. This level of pain has manifested itself as self-hatred and is projected outward onto another brother. Among young kings, homicide is a form of suicide because the victim is killed and the offenders life is destroyed through incarceration. This phenomenon supports the old clinical adage "hurt people hurt people."

Those artists that perform and promote this destructive subculture are celebrated and heavily rewarded by the media and music industry. This kind of exultation of those artists and producers causes millions of kings around the world to not only want to be like them, but emulate their dress, style, and reinforce negative values. Nowadays, toxic rap artists have so much popularity and fame that they are idolized by many young kings. This places the artist in a position of power in which they can create trends and influence a mass of people.

Music Used As Psychological Warfare

In many of our communities, toxic rappers have more influence than parents, preachers, and teachers—especially those who are in impoverished areas. Using music and negative programming subconsciously alters awareness, thoughts, beliefs, and behaviors (*Psychology Today*, 2012). Those beliefs influence values and promote a subculture that is the opposite of all that is right and encourages sociopathic behaviors. Over the years, I have encountered hundreds of young kings that have been poisoned by lyrics that cause a moral decline and influence them to make poor decisions.

I often use music therapy and other unique interventions in my school-based clinic with young kings. Many of the young kings placed in the alternative school setting met diagnostic criteria for Oppositional Defiant Disorder and Conduct Disorder. When introducing music therapy, I would ask young kings to name their favorite song and play it on YouTube during a session to build rapport. This provides a communal experience in which they are allowed to express themselves musically. I would often bop to the music as well to show an appreciation for the soundtrack.

During this process, I am gathering information and observing body language, facial expressions, breathing patterns, and most of all, listening to content. During the assessment process, about 95% of the participants would name a rap song promoting self-destructive behaviors and criminality. While playing their favorite track, I have observed young kings go into a transcendental state with their eyes closed, reciting destructive and murderous lyrics as if it was a form of worship. After the music ends, we would process and discuss line by line each act, command, and celebratory statement that is clearly negative and destructive. This often redirects the young king and causes them to think about behaviors and beliefs that are clearly unacceptable.

After being redirected several times with support, they would often yield and acknowledge how the toxic lyrics had a subliminal effect on their thought process. I also impress upon them the laws of nature, which

69

simply attest to a man reaping what he sowed. These types of interventions not only appeal to the innermost conscience of the young
king, but also worked well in building rapport. Overcoming barriers
in treatment are very important because, traditionally, African Americans have not been receptive to mental health services and counseling.
Once a rapport is established, the young king realizes how the lyrics
affect their thoughts and perceptions. This process is very important
because many of them are not aware of the impact music has on the
mind. This type of consistent programming causes the development
of a persona or false self, which often leads to criminality or self-sabo-
taging behaviors.

This is the reason why the scientific community mandated a rating
system that we now know as G, PG, R, and X to provide some sense
of awareness and censorship to those that were consuming media and
music productions. Nowadays, the rag is off the bush and profit takes
priority over health and wellness, especially as it relates to the well-be-
ing of young kings.

Another one of my interventions used with young kings is the "picture me rolling" exercise, inspired by a rap song by Tupac Shakur.
Tupac started the track by commanding the audience to picture him
rolling in a 500 Benz. He was not only visualizing but willing a reality
into existence. Within my school-based clinic, many of the referrals and
redirection would be for dress code violations and sagging pants. There
were so many young kings getting in trouble for the same offense that
I had to become creative in my interventions.

The "picture me rolling" intervention would be used when young kings would get in trouble for sagging or violating the dress code. Once I identified the target behavior, which was sagging, I would then encourage them to relax and breathe deeply with their eyes closed. Then, I'd use guided imagery techniques to assist him in creating powerful images of himself. Guided imagery is a therapeutic exercise in which the client is given vivid instructions in formulating an imaginary reality.

I would ask the young king if they wanted to have a nuclear family one day, and the vast majority would respond yes. If answered in affirmative, I would then ask him to imagine being a proud king, living in a castle, with a queen as your wife, prince, and princess as children. With their eyes closed, the vision of kingship would often cause the young king to smile outwardly.

In the next phase, I would ask him if he could imagine himself running around the castle with sagging pants and his underwear exposed to his wife and children. In shame and in privacy, they would always shake their heads, answering "no." This response let me know that in their hearts, they knew they were wrong; however, the desire to be accepted and affirmed influenced how they dressed. Many young kings simply have no alternative way of obtaining validation among peers other than assimilating to a negative dress code despite the consequences.

The conclusion of the exercise almost always ended with them pulling their pants up in my presence. The sad part about it is once they returned to the environment, many of them would default back to sagging a couple of days later because of the negative peer pressure. I have also encountered incidents in which some of the young kings couldn't pull their pants up because they were too small. In this case, pulling their pants up would make them the object of ridicule. I then realized that it was not only a peer pressure issue. Many of them were sagging because they didn't have adequate clothing. As a parent of three young kings, pants are often the second most expensive clothing item other than their sneakers. As a matter of a fact, I have had to buy more jeans than sneakers because of the growth spurts during adolescence. These occurrences caused me to form a hypothesis. I wondered if some of the young kings were wearing pants too small or too big out of necessity rather than fashion.

Often, the most disadvantaged youth can impact culture and fashion to set trends and make almost anything cool. I paid close attention to the dress of some of the most impoverished adolescents and realized many of them were wearing clothing that they had either outgrown or didn't belong to them. This kind of adaptation allows adolescents to wear clothing too big or too small and escape ridicule while being accepted among peers.

As a child, I remember peers being joked and clowned because they had what we called "reject shoes" or "high waters." It was of great importance that you could dress and have name-brand shoes. Nowadays, things have gotten worse because of social media and excessive materialism. The same adaptation was used by inner-city youth that didn't have access to instruments in the 1980s and started a musical art form known as beat-boxing. These types of adaptations are clear examples of how creative and intelligent our youth are, especially those that are disadvantaged.

I also noticed a trend of young kings wearing hoods in the building as a dress code violation. While in session, I would ask them to remove their hoods, and they would often respond by saying, "I need a haircut." The same is true with encountering young kings wearing a pair of Jordans that were two sizes too small and suffering from the pain of wearing the shoe. These types of experiences shed light upon the multiple challenges that are mounted against young kings that we may sometimes view as defiance or disrespect. Many young kings are being influenced by a subculture that leads to only two places. Those two places are, as the elders would say, "The jailhouse or an early grave."

This kind of maladaptive coping mechanism also applies when assimilating to negative values within the subculture. This also creates a form of cognitive dissonance in the young king. Cognitive dissonance theory suggests that a person cannot be at peace unless their beliefs and values are in alignment. For example, a murderer cannot be at peace and kill people unless they change their beliefs and feel they are justified or right for killing. As a therapist who understands how impressionable adolescents are in forming beliefs at this stage, I would spend much of my time countering negative beliefs and values that are self-destructive and counterproductive. I always encourage and affirm the reality that they too can be successful. I impress upon them it is possible if they have a realistic plan, work hard, apply the proper principles, and keep the faith.

As a young king growing up in the 1990s, we had a balance of positive rappers that could provide a healthy balance by promoting positive values. For example, I can recall positive artists such as Outkast, The Goodie Mob,

Nas, and KRS 1. These were artists that provided insight, instruction, and correction through their musical programming. During my freshman year in college, I remember listening to these artists and being empowered. You couldn't walk through the dormitory of Claflin College without hearing rap music that taught pearls of wisdom and cultivated a positive self-concept.

My classmates and I would have group sessions in which we would discuss many of the powerful lessons and information delivered through the music. This positive programming was very instrumental and sparked a level of consciousness that assisted us in our development. The messages were always uplifting, insightful, and motivational. This type of positive programming was especially needed because it was able to counter some of the gangster rap and negative media programming that was growing in influence.

Then, around 1995, a lot of new emerging rap artists shifted their themes and content from being positive to a thug life culture. There was an explosion of artists who celebrated violence, ignorance, and social disobedience. The rap culture shifted from dancing, having fun, and being wise to destructive messages that were commanding us to kill, get high, rob, and disrespect women. This negative programming influenced our dress, speech, and the way we interacted with other young kings. This cultural shift was so powerful that many of my peers wanted to be like them, talk like them, and act like them.

This created an environment in which if you were not "gangster," you were considered as being weak or lame. This persona encouraged negative behaviors, such as drinking a 40-ounce of malt liquor, smoking weed, and being willing to use deadly force against someone who looked like you gained momentum. Suddenly, it was like the values taught by our elders were in reverse. Those that were negative were socially rewarded and those that were positive were ridiculed or targeted.

Rap music morphed into a powerful tool to program Black men with self-destructive values. I witnessed many young males become products of negative programming by not only celebrating the gangster/thug lifestyle but also practicing it. In hindsight, we were not aware of the psychological effect the music had on our minds as young kings. Music alters moods, thoughts, and belief systems. I watched many young men fall victim to a program designed to destroy them without their consent. They were contaminated by negative programming that was forced upon them by a toxic subculture.

Young kings who do not have positive male support and have economic challenges are especially at risk of being programmed by rap poison. Those young kings that don't have strong male role models often look to the toxic rap artist to be their idols. This is a major problem because those rappers who have been exalted by the media and subculture are typically the most violent and uneducated. Many artists are consumed with trying to get "the bag" or "get rich or die trying." Even if a rap artist is not violent or uneducated, they must portray an image that supports negative behaviors to become marketable in an industry driven by profit. This type of programming through media productions is a type of psychological warfare that poisons the minds of young kings.

Toxic rap artists are rewarded and celebrated for poisoning young kings with no kind of consequence other than becoming a victim of the subculture themselves. Nowadays, being a rap artist is one of the most hazardous occupations a young king can have. In the past 35 years, there have been over 93 famous rappers that have been killed. Even though these numbers may be alarming, we cannot even imagine how many young kings have been impacted by this form of psychological programming by committing murder, being murdered, being incarcerated, or becoming addicted to illicit drugs.

This kind of negative programming not only influences the young kings, but it also contaminates our females of African descent. Many young queens are also being influenced to reward those young kings that identify with this poisonous subculture. This is a powerful dynamic because the most aggressive young kings provide her with a false sense of safety and protection within pressured environments. The young queens are being programmed as well to desire the males that are most violent and cool. I counseled young queens and discovered that many of them are attracted to the young king that emulates the hottest rapper or entertainer.

During their adolescent stages, many young queens cannot understand the dangers and liabilities associated with these types of relationships. These types of dynamics within the male-female relationship must be addressed, as it leads to further dysfunction. Dysfunction between young kings and queens not only affects their relationships, but it also contributes to the destruction of the Black family system.

While I am sure toxic rap is not our only problem, it is a recipe for disaster when coupled with poverty and self-destructive programming. As a helping professional, my primary job is to support, promote healing, and bring awareness to patterns or behaviors that may be harmful to the public. Again, toxic rap music reinforces negative values that must be addressed and further explored by the scientific community. This has been a public service announcement, and it is my ethical responsibility to warn.

The dangers of social media and artificial intelligence

We live in an ever-changing world that has no boundaries because of modern technology and social media. It is common to see children as young as three years old with tablets or playing with cell phones. Children can become addicted or contaminated by images that are not fit for human consumption during the most impressionable years of their lives. It is very important to limit screen time and censor programming, especially during the early stages of development.

A child's brain is growing rapidly and is vulnerable to overstimulation. Many of the programs and games have been designed to be addictive and enslave their consumers. There are many tech companies that are under major scrutiny for encouraging their engineers to develop games that cause the reward center of the brain to release dopamine in response to a pleasurable experience or hyperarousal. This is one reason we have seen an increase in attention deficit disorder (ADHD). Children that are always on tech devices are being overly stimulated and are seeking to find pleasure rewards continuously. A survey of tech use during the COVID-19 pandemic revealed increased screen time ramped up other mental health issues, such as anxiety, a lack of interest in other school activities, and sleeping problems. The overuse of tech devices and video games has similar effects on the brain as addictive drugs. They both trigger the release of dopamine in the pleasure reward system and create dependence. For this reason, parents should be very careful about introducing electronic devices that provide access to the world uncensored.

I have worked with countless families whose children had been exposed to hard pornography, violence, and drugs through media consumption without parental awareness. This type of negative media exposure often leads to experimentation, or the reproduction of behaviors observed. Keep in mind, a child doesn't have the ability to understand the difference between falsehood and reality. Nowadays, with the emergence of reality TV shows, even adults have challenges with the same concept, so you can only imagine how it can affect a child's mind.

Many children's minds are being attacked by artificial intelligence/robots that have been designed to create dependence for profit. And yes, I said it, electronic devices are robots being powered by programs. These platforms are influenced by your inquiries and designed to be addictive so that they can profit from suggestive marketing. For example, if a child is on TikTok and they see someone fighting and pause before swiping, artificial intelligence identifies it as a topic of interest. The pause before swiping lets the robot know you have an interest in the image presented.

The algorithm/program will send them more images of violent content that influences aggressive behaviors and social attitudes.

Within my practice, I have witnessed adolescents within a school setting watch video recordings of people being shot, murdered, or viciously assaulted in living color while laughing at the images. This desensitizes youth and causes them to normalize such behaviors. This is one factor that influences an increase in school shootings and violent acts committed by youth. Whatever you have an appetite for, artificial intelligence will increase your exposure, whether you are conscious are not.

In China, their government has implemented strict censorship of children's exposure to TikTok despite them being the creators of the program. Children under 14 are limited to consuming educational and patriotic videos. Many parents have fallen victim to allowing their children early access to cell phones, tablets, and social media with minimal oversight and supervision. This new trend took the whole world by storm, and the masses were intoxicated with all the freedom and information. I have evaluated children with video game and porn addictions as early as nine years old. Cell phones became so common, we forgot that they not only have games but also provide unlimited access to negative information and programming.

America failed to reinforce the importance of censorship in the media, especially for children. In 1934, "The Hays Code" was a self-imposed industry guideline for all motion pictures released between 1934 and 1968. The code prohibited nudity, profanity, and graphic or realistic violence. Even back then, the entertainment industry knew all information disseminated through media was a type of programming that would influence human behavior.

They did this under the pressure of the scientific community to protect the minds of its citizens, especially children. Children and adolescents are especially vulnerable because they cannot properly determine fact from fiction. Nowadays, the "rag is off the bush" and there is zero censorship or parental supervision in the consumption of music, gaming, and media. This leaves our youths' minds in the hands of those who do not have our best interests at heart. As parents or caregivers, we must do all that we can to protect our children's minds from all media and images that will not have a positive effect on their development.

The Cultivation of Positive Self-Concept

T he cultivation of positive self-concept is one of the most powerful things that you can provide for a young king. In the 1990s, people of color had a variety of positive programming that created a space to cultivate Black excellence. *The Cosby Show* and *A Different World* had a profound effect on an entire generation. In fact, this kind of positive imagery changed the trajectory of our culture in the media and inspired many Black youths to attend college and become professionals.

Nowadays, the media is practically void of positive programming for young kings and this places the responsibility primarily on the caregivers. Often, the caregiver is not conscious of the negative forces that are attacking our young kings' minds. It is of great importance that we begin to question and evaluate our own parenting methods, so that we may always adapt, adjust, and monitor for best outcomes.

As people of African descent, much of our culture has been hijacked and poisoned to the point where our young kings are being punished and ridiculed for being smart and articulate. This destructive subculture of ignorance has become a dominant force and causes many young kings to emulate artists or athletes rather than become strong young men with purpose and character. This is not an attempt to stereotype males of African descent; however, throughout my years of experience, many young kings suffer from an identity crisis that affects their development in some way.

For example, I have worked with numerous young kings that felt as if they had to hide the fact that their father was in their lives or if they lived in a middle-class community. Many of them would be ridiculed or called "spoon-fed or soft" because they have certain advantages. The subculture and media reinforce a narrative that is powerful because it rewards those that are negative and punishes those that are positive. If you are not from the streets, you are soft or uncool. If a young king is perceived as being soft or uncool in a pressured environment, it often causes them to become a target and are often victimized or bullied. This subculture is so powerful that it causes many young kings to change their values so they can survive in a pressured environment and have a negative impact on their self-concept.

The lack of positive self-concept cripples young kings and extends their adolescent stage into young adulthood. Unfortunately, this is why many males of African descent still act like juveniles when they are in their 20s and 30s. You can literally take these same men, place them in a high school, and they would blend well. Their speech, dress, and mentality would be similar because of a subculture that celebrates and reinforces these behaviors. Many young kings subconsciously try to emulate artists and entertainers without understanding the artists are simply marketing a brand that supports them and their families.

Many of the artists and athletes have the resources to insulate them from having to assimilate into the dominant culture. So, to be clear, many young kings fall victim to subliminal programming, not under-standing their swag will make them undesirable and pose as a barrier in the workforce. This doesn't mean that young kings should strive to assimilate to European culture; however, a man who wears his pants below the equator will not be considered for employment in many institutions nor would he be taken seriously as a businessman.

Cultural awareness and history are important elements in developing a positive view of oneself. A young king should have a positive percep-tion of himself and his people. This will require that we research and share African contributions to civilization pre- and post-enslavement. Throughout American history, people of African descent have been portrayed as subservient, savage, or used strictly for entertainment. There has been much effort devoted toward stealing our culture and dehumanizing people of African descent within America.

As a young king, I struggled with a positive self-concept because of a lack of exposure to our history. It affected how I viewed myself and the world around me. In fact, all the institutions I had ever known were controlled and dominated by Europeans except for the church and the barbershops. They were minuscule compared to the grocery stores, hospitals, dealerships, and industries in which people of color were employed. This inferiority complex followed me through high school. I barely graduated and couldn't see myself attending college.

At seventeen, my mother put pressure on me to either go into the military or college. The mother eagle stirred the nest. I didn't want to go into the military, so I told her I would attend college. The next day, I went to school and informed my guidance counselor of my plans to attend college. She smirked and said, "You are not college material." Then, she instructed me to train for a manufacturing job.

I came home and told my mother what she said, and she replied, "We will get you into school." When August came around, I thought she was going to let me stay at home. I remember it like it was yesterday. I was in the bathroom, and she yelled through the door with her Gullah Geechee dialect... "What are you gonna do, buddy, college or military?" I was scared and looked on the dresser and ironically saw a college brochure that had some Black students on the front, and it was from Claflin College, now known as Claflin University.

This was ironic because I never applied to or knew anything about HBCUs. She said, "Okay, I will take you to Orangeburg next week." Even though we were poor, my family was proud. She dropped me off, gave me $5 per week, and told me to make my way. I was scared, and I didn't believe I could graduate from college. My plan was to attend for a few semesters and return home and get a job in a plant after failing. That was my mindset; I simply couldn't see myself earning a college degree based on my experiences and background.

There I was, a first-generation college student, scared, and knew that I was going to fail. One day, I walked across the railroad tracks on Golf

Avenue to get some chips. I noticed a bum with long matted dreadlocks, wearing a colorful shirt. Fighting down fear, I shook my head in disbelief.

I arrived in class the next day and was surprised to see that the man I thought was a bum was Dr. Jones. Dr. Jones had a Ph.D. and taught African Studies and Geography. It was then that my perception of myself and my people evolved. I wanted to learn more and entertained the possibility of becoming a scholar myself. In African studies class, Dr. Jones taught us about ancient African history. As one of the most notable instructors, he had a profound impact on my self-concept. I learned about Imhotep, the original father of medicine. He was an architect credited for building the step pyramids, a physician, and a priest. He came into prominence from 2650 BC to 2600 during the 13th dynasty. Imhotep predated western medicine and Hippocrates by 2200 years. A Black Egyptian, the Greeks revered and worshiped him as the *God of Medicine* because of his ability to diagnose and treat ailments.

Learning about my history as a teenager was very inspirational and caused me to imagine the psychological effect it could have had on me as a child. This is the reason why African contributions to civilization were hidden throughout western history. In the words of Frederick Douglass, "*knowledge makes a man unfit to be a slave*". Learning about "black excellence" made me perceive myself as being intelligent and sparked my thirst for knowledge.

We must teach our young kings about their legacy of greatness, so they can take their rightful place. It is also critical we teach our young kings that our history didn't begin with slavery. It is this power construct that inspired me to become a practitioner, scientist, and author. We came from greatness and must equip our young kings with the understanding of who they are to prevent them from having an inferiority complex.

Many of the social ills that African descendants of slaves now are suffering from are merely the results of a lack of knowledge. It is important that we deprogram all the negative information forced upon us and reprogram our young kings with all that is needed to develop a positive self-concept.

Manhood

When I was a child, I spoke as a child, I understood as a child, I thought as a child: but when I became a man, I put away childish things. 1 corinthians 13-11

Manhood is a subject that is sadly debated and has become so watered down that many are not able to clearly define its essence. So, within this chapter, I will provide a simple definition. A man is a mature biological male of the human species. Manhood is the exemplification of qualities associated with men, which is distinguished from a child or a female. While these are broad and ambiguous definitions, it is important that we have some kind of context.

Within this book, I have thoroughly presented many of the barriers that hinder young kings from developing into responsible, well-adjusted men, including a lack of male role models and negative programming. While we know these dynamics have a tremendous effect, I believe a single woman can support and teach a male child the principles of manhood with community support. While many people complain about the lack of positive Black role models in America, there are always strong men of color who are more than willing to assist young kings who are humble.

We ARE Our Brother's Keeper

If a young king is respectful, he will never have a problem finding mentors or male support. Good men will see those qualities shining in the darkness and be drawn to it. Whenever men encounter a young king who is willing to learn, the experience is not a burden. Instead, it is an honorable responsibility.

I have been on the receiving and giving side of the table. I have had many good men help me along my way. I refer to them as mentors or elders who were sprinkled throughout my life to assist me or teach valuable lessons. Some of them were coaches, coworkers, ministers, or random men God sent specifically to help me. Many times, men of color get a bad rap for not helping our youth; however, this is far from the truth.

One of the biggest issues in mentoring youth is that many of them are not ready for mentorship. Instead, they need to be trained. A young king who is not trained can be dangerous and requires too much energy. Training is the parent's or caregiver's job, not the community. It is the parent's job to teach the child to be respectful, and of good character. Nowadays, men of color are fearful to say anything to those young kings who are not trained for fear of being harmed. The lack of home training poses as a barrier that will discourage wise men from engaging them. Just because a man is not in the home doesn't mean a young king can't be trained.

Most times throughout African American history, the Black woman has had to train and cultivate young kings into strong men. For example, we have seen countless incidents in which mothers, grandmothers, and aunties have been primarily responsible for raising great men. In fact, I really don't believe a man can reach his full potential without a good woman in his life. Even though a woman cannot teach a male how to be a man, they *can* teach and support the child in grasping the principles of manhood. In fact, my mother taught me and my brothers many of the manhood principles that have guided me into manhood. In reflection, it was almost like she built us to be what she believed a good man should be to care for a wife and children. While my father was present throughout my life, he allowed my mother to take leadership most times because she had learned things from her father that even he had not been taught by his father.

While my father provided a positive example of how a man is supposed to carry himself, my mother helped to teach and discipline us with a stern hand, as if she knew what we were going to encounter as men.

She would always drive home principles of manhood by telling us what a man should do and what a man shouldn't do. She always emphasized the importance of qualities such as pride, courage, dignity, respect, work ethic, sacrifice, and wisdom. Some principles and instructions were:

A man is supposed to be wise; a man without wisdom is a fool.

A man is supposed to be righteous; you will reap what you sow.

A man is supposed to take care of his family; it is not your wife's responsibility to provide.

A man is supposed to be proud; always carry yourself in a respectable manner.

A man will never own a woman; she can always choose to render her services somewhere else.

Men don't play. If men horseplay, it will result in someone getting hurt.

And finally, son, a man will kill you over a woman.

These were some of the principles or laws she drove home to me and my brothers as early as I can remember. While I know some people may consider these principles to be obsolete or even primitive, these are the expectations and values that cultivated me as a man. They also serve as a template and a guide that can be shared intergenerationally. Nowadays, it is disturbing to see young kings show little qualities of manliness. In these cases, it is clear they are in rebellion or have not been trained. Males who have not been trained to respect authority, especially during adolescence, often result in being overly emotional and undisciplined. Because of the absence of positive manhood training, we have witnessed the emergence of immature males or masculinity that is commonly described as toxic. Toxic masculinity is a term used to describe men devoid of the ability to control their emotions and respect others. The term is also misused to neutralize or control manliness when it doesn't align with a distorted feminist agenda.

The best way I have heard masculinity described is being likened to a sword in its sheath. The one who carries it can be a warrior; however, he has the self-control and civility to live in peace. There is an old saying that asserts "No one appreciates the warrior until the enemy is at the gates." As men, we understand the primary thing that makes a man respect one another is that we can set boundaries and enforce them if necessary. For example, if a man comes into another man's home and smacks his wife on her behind in front of his children, there is a serious possibility, things could get violent. In fact, if the man didn't respond assertively to protect his wife, then she and his children would lose respect for him.

This is simply how nature works. Men have been biologically designed to be protectors and providers. This is the reason the Creator has gifted them with higher levels of testosterone and larger muscle mass. There has been a war waged against Black masculinity, and it must be addressed on all fronts. The only way we can win this war is if we understand it is our responsibility to teach, support, and train our young kings to be men. While manhood training is a tedious journey, it is important to remember that you *can* do it. If young kings reached their full potential as men in America, what would be the consequence in our communities?

Financial Literacy

E conomical discrimination and a lack of financial literacy are the primary reasons males of African descent catch hell in America. One of the hardest things a young king will encounter is being able to accumulate enough resources for himself and his family. Throughout history, people of African descent have been exploited for their labor through chattel slavery. Slavery was an economical institution in which Whites benefited from the free labor of enslaved Africans.

The torture and inhumane treatment were simply instruments used to maintain power and control of the machine that built America. The European settlers came from a land that was overcrowded and less desirable in search of life, livelihood, and the pursuit of property. Property was defined as enslaved Africans, land, and tools. Thomas Jefferson later revised the creed by replacing it with "Life, Liberty, and the Pursuit of Happiness..." which was in The Declaration of Independence of 1776.

Switching the pursuit of property to happiness was done to disguise the theft of land from the indigenous people and shift the focus on an emotional construct. Happiness can't be weighed, measured, or quantified, as it is an emotion that often depends on how you feel. The pursuit of property was the primary goal for European settlers, and all others would be considered a servant class. After slavery ended, this created a shift because people of color were no longer assets. Instead, they were liabilities because they could no longer be exploited for free labor.

There was such a dramatic change in the American economy the American government implemented more racist and unfair policies that enriched White families and left African Americans in the dust. One of the most destructive policies post-slavery was redlining. Redlining was implemented at the end of the 1930s after the Great Depression during the housing crisis. A new federal organization was formed called the Homeowners Loan Association. This new entity created a zoning map that had non-white communities outlined in red and denied funding based on their location. This denied millions of people of color from building wealth and home ownership.

In contrast, the White neighborhoods were fully funded and granted low-interest rates to homes with federal funds. Redlining was not outlawed until the 1968 Fair Housing Act; however, the damage was done. I always wondered why there was such a drastic difference between White neighborhoods and Black neighborhoods. In many of our cities, you can simply cross the railroad tracks and enter communities of color that appear as though they have been abandoned or in a war zone. This practice not only stopped Black families from passing on generational wealth, but it also left our communities in poverty.

The Bitter Fruit of Poverty

Poverty puts you in jeopardy of suffering from every social ill under the sun and often leads to criminality. Those who are poor are more likely to have lower life expectancies, suffer from addictions, and become victims of violent crimes. They are also more likely to be incarcerated. So, when you couple poverty with racial discrimination, it has a debilitating effect that cripples our communities of color.

According to a recent study in 2019, before the COVID-19 pandemic, it was estimated that Black Americans had one-sixth the wealth of White Americans on an average per capita basis. This means for every dollar, the average White American has, the average Black American has only about 17 cents. Also, for every dollar that the median White family has, the median Black American family has 10 cents. These numbers clearly reveal a major disparity in the amount of wealth in America.

It is critical to note that the pandemic has accelerated wealth concentration and negatively impacted Black and Latino communities attempting to grapple with the aftereffects of COVID-19. It is of great importance that we prepare our young kings by equipping them with the tools necessary to thrive in a capitalistic society. While there are many barriers that stand in our way, we must also teach them sound economic principles. As a young scholar, becoming immersed in all the research and history that shed light on the powers of systematic racial discrimination, it was almost paralyzing. I was compelled to focus my research efforts on finding a solution that might assist our kings in being successful in America and defy all the negative statistics and stereotypes.

My research topic was "Relationships Between Perceived Racial Discrimination and Self-Efficacy: The Roles of Race, Gender, and Resilience." Within my research, I proved that perceived racial discrimination has a tremendous effect on a young king's level of self-efficacy and resilience. To clarify my point, self-efficacy is the belief in a person's ability to execute behaviors and achieve goals. Resilience is the capacity to withstand or recover from difficulties. It was discovered within my research that perceived racial discrimination has a negative effect on the strength of self-efficacy and resilience. The traumatic effect of racial discrimination is so powerful that many young kings lose faith, which prevents them from believing in themselves and giving up.

I have encountered hundreds of young kings who are so broken by a system of racial discrimination they won't even try to succeed. It's almost like giving a man a lawnmower and gas with an operational manual; however, he won't attempt to cut the grass because he's convinced that he's going to fail despite having all the tools he needs. Therefore, we must be aggressive in strengthening young kings' levels of self-efficacy and resilience through programming and support.

Despite all these challenges African Americans face, there is still hope. In 2021, Black spending power reached a record 1.6 trillion dollars. African Americans have historically held an extremely powerful position in the retail marketplace, as they have driven trends across food, beauty, media, and more. Their influence will continue to grow as their buying power does, which is projected to reach $1.8 trillion by 2024.

This information lets us know that we have the resources; however, they are not being properly managed and delegated as a group. Therefore, financial literacy is important, especially among our young kings. Nowadays, American poverty can be considered a condition influenced by financial value deficits. There is no doubt racial discrimination exists in America. Still, if you learn sound principles and are disciplined in applying them, you can become financially secure.

We live in one of the richest countries in the world, yet the face of poverty can be hidden behind designer clothes, $200 sneakers, and luxury vehicles. This negative subculture of celebrating spending money frivolously is reinforced by the media and entertainment industry. I'm sure that you have seen images of young kings on social media flashing racks and stacks of cash. This topic of discussion hits home for me because I was born in poverty and spent much of my young adulthood suffering from its effects. I found myself being influenced by the same subculture as a young adult. I simply didn't have the knowledge or awareness to break the cycle of poverty. I remember buying luxury vehicles and clothing to feel a sense of self-worth among my peers while renting a place to live. Later in life, the consequences of such behaviors caught up with me and I realized I was poor, and my family would suffer if I didn't change my values and behaviors. I was fortunate to meet mentors that taught me the basic principles of delayed gratification, finances, and credit. Until then, I didn't know what to do with my money. Peers and rap poison heavily influenced me to squander every dollar I earned on liabilities that symbolize wealth.

Financial literacy should be taught as early as elementary school and caregivers should practice sound economic principles so that they not only teach but practice the principles themselves. This requires that you, as a parent/caregiver, learn new concepts as well. Many parents pass on a legacy of ignorance and poverty simply because they themselves haven't been educated. As a caregiver of young kings, we must help them develop a basic understanding of how vital economics is to their survival. Financial literacy is not taught in our public school systems, nor is it taught within our institutions of higher learning. Therefore, it must come from you.

If you don't have a clue where to begin, I strongly encourage you to consider investing in Dr. Boyce Watkins' financial curriculum for youth: The 15 Things Every Black Child Needs to Know About Money. Dr. Boyce Watkins is an African American economist that has devoted his life to the financial education and upliftment of people of color. Within his program, young kings will be taught the basic principles of finances and wealth building. Not only should we teach our young kings financial literacy, but much effort should also be devoted to teaching discipline and delayed gratification.

Delayed gratification is a challenge, especially for young kings nowadays, because everything is instant and fast. No one wants to wait because they want it now. The media and modern technology have handicapped us to expect instant gratification. I remember when we had to wait for our favorite show to come on television. Now, things are on demand without delay. This kind of instant gratification has tricked the adolescent mind to see time as a barrier instead of a friend.

For example, I've asked many young kings if they would rather have $100,000 now or $1 million in 10 years. The vast majority would respond by saying give me the 100 stacks now because they cannot see that far in the future and often believe that they could invest or flip it into a million in a shorter period. In this case, time is an enemy because their minds cannot comprehend waiting because of youth and circumstance. They want to have experiences in the present that will not benefit them in the future. One of the best lessons you can teach a young king is the ability to delay gratification. This is not only an issue that affects African American males however the consequences are more severe because of racial discrimination and income disparities.

When educating young kings about financial literacy, we often neglect to explain the importance of group economics. Group economics can be as simple as getting married to the right partner, so the two may achieve economic goals. Marriage was primarily meant to be an economical institution in which two people could pool their resources and care for offspring. This is a system that still works today. There is so much that can be accomplished if people of African descent go back to the basics.

I have assisted many young kings in creating a life plan; however, only a few are willing to make sacrifices and follow a plan. With that being said, I am reminded of The Gospel according to Rayquan.

Rayquan was a nineteen-year-old male of African descent who had just graduated from high school in South Carolina. He was not the coolest guy, so the ladies never really gave him any play in school. However, he had the desire to get married and have a family. After deciding college was not for him, he started working at a local factory making $13 per hour. The work was hard, and he had to endure freezing temperatures loading boxes of poultry in an industrial-size freezer. To help him out, his mother allowed him to stay home if he paid the utility bills.

The first year, he saved $9,000 and bought a used Toyota truck for $7,000, while many of his friends who worked with him purchased Dodge Chargers. Most of his friends were in college partying or working without a plan and squandering their money. The second year he received a $2 raise and was promoted to another department because of his work ethic and willingness to pull extra shifts for his supervisor. The money was good, but the promotion required that he work overtime and swing shifts. Rayquan saved $15,000 in his second year. In the third and fourth years, he saved $30,000. This gave him a total of $45,000.

He was now twenty-two years old and remembered his mentor saying, "Real estate is the best way to build wealth and secure your family." He began his search for distressed properties. This was during the housing crisis of 2008, so the housing market was hot for cash buyers. Rayquan purchased a foreclosed property with cash for $32,000.

It needed a lot of work, he took his time and used $10,000 of his savings to fix it up. It appraised one year later at $82,000. Rayquan was debt-free, with a house and truck paid for while in his early twenties. He began dating and met a young lady named Tonya. Tonya was a late bloomer as well. Rayquan appreciated that she was trustworthy, supportive, and reliable. She wasn't the least bit interested in fads and trends.

In other words, Tonya would have been considered as being *"basic."* She had no desire to get her nails done, wear designer clothing, or go out with her girlfriends. She had a sense of what she wanted out of life: a family. Rayquan knew she was the right one because she had been consistent throughout their relationship, and they worked together to achieve their goals. Tonya was finishing college and wanted to be a teacher. They hit it off well and decided to explore marriage. While they were dating, he had come up with another plan because his responsibilities and vision had grown.

Rayquan developed a solid financial plan with Tonya. He told her that it would require them to delay gratification and sacrifice for five years. He calculated the figures and realized both could save around $40,000 per year with her teaching salary and his income since they had no house payment. The plan was to invest their income in rental properties. Tonya was hesitant, however, she believed in him and trusted Rayquan because of his character.

Rayquan and Tonya got married, and the only expenses they had were her small car payment of $205.00, food, and utilities. At first, it was a challenge because all her peers and family were living life by traveling, buying designer clothing, cars, and posting on Instagram. Rayquan noticed how Instagram was affecting her and jokingly said with affection, "Sweetheart, Instagram is simply a tool many people use to instantly show their a$$, it's nobody's business what you eat or where you are going." After that serious but playful conversation, Tonya decided to unplug from social media and distanced herself from negative influences.

They implemented the plan and caught hell buying and fixing up those properties; however, God blessed them to find two properties for around $30,000. At the end of five years, they had accumulated seven rental properties with their primary home paid off. Those years flew by, and she didn't realize what they accomplished until Rayquan came home with some flowers and said congratulations honey.

She asked what the occasion was, and he told her that they had exceeded their goal and wanted to celebrate by taking a vacation. They decided to take a trip to Jamaica during the New Year's holiday. While at dinner in Jamaica, on a cliff overlooking the ocean, Tonya asked him what's next. Rayquan told her they could begin having the children they always wanted. He told her she could stop teaching and focus on the children and manage the rental properties.

Tonya was elated; however, she told him she couldn't do that because he would still have to work in those harsh conditions, and his feet were in terrible shape from working in freezing temperatures on those wet concrete floors. He smirked and asked the waiter for a pen and listed each property with $6,300 per month in residual rental income. Rayquan also shared their primary home increased in value to $130,000. He proposed they refinance their primary residence to build their dream home for more space and access to better schools. He also informed her he was going to obtain his general contractor's license and start his new career in real estate. Tonya became tearful and laughed with joy. Tonya and Rayquan became millionaires before the age of 30. Each house appraised at an average of

$125,000 after five years. They built their dream home and had three children. Tonya and Rayquan lived happily ever after. The End.

This story is an example of how a sound financial plan, work ethic, sacrifice, patience, and discipline can enable you to achieve your goals and build generational wealth. While America has its shortcomings and challenges, it remains a place in which nightmares can become sweet dreams. This story was inspired by true events.

In conclusion, I know I have shared a lot of information in this book that I hope will be useful on your journey. Even though I have referenced many struggles you will experience as a caregiver of a young king in America, it is important that I remind you that you can do it. Keep the faith and stay engaged. The greater the trial, the larger the crown.

About the Author

D r. Terrance Wells is a native of Sumter, South Carolina. He has over twenty-six years of human service experience specializing in working with adolescents and families. He obtained a bachelor's degree from Claflin University in Sociology, a Master of Education with an emphasis in Counseling Psychology from Troy University and a PhD in General Psychology from Capella University. He holds three clinical licenses as a Professional Counselor, Professional Counselor Supervisor, and Licensed Addictions Counselor. Dr. Wells is certified in six psychological disciplines and has devoted his life to serving people in their time of need.

In his free time, Dr. Wells enjoys spending time with his family and friends. His secret talent is that he can sing but won't if requested.

Appendix

DeGruy Leary, J. (2005) Post Traumatic Slave Syndrome: America's Legacy of Enduring Injury and Healing.

Anderson, Claud. (1994) Black Labor White Wealth: The Search for Power and Economic Justice.

Kunjufu, K. (1983) The Conspiracy to Destroy Black Males.

DuBois, W.E.B (1903) The Souls Of Black Folk

Cheikh Anta Diop (1974)The African Origin of Civilization: Myth or Reality.

Wilson, Amos (1993) The Falsification of Afrikan Consciousness

Fontanella CA, Steelesmith DL, Brock G, Bridge JA, Campo JV, Fristad MA. Association of Cannabis Use With Self-harm and Mortality Risk Among Youths With Mood Disorders. *JAMA Pediatr.* 2021;175(4):377–384. doi:10.1001/jamapediatrics.2020.5494

Hennekens, C. Mortality, Drowos, J, Levine, R (2013) Mortality from Homicide among Young Black Men: American Tragedy.

Potter, L. (1998). Influence of homicide on racial disparity in life expectancy–United States.

MMWR Morb Mortal Wkly Rep. 2001; 50: 780-782

David C. Ribar, Why Marriage Matters for Child Wellbeing," *The Future of Children*, 25:2 (Fall 2015), 23.

Devries, R. (2000). Vygotsky, piaget, and education: a reciprocal assimilation of theories and educational practices. New Ideas in Psychology

24 (U.S. Bureau of Labor Statistics, November 2014), https://www.bls.gov/opub/btn/volume-3/income-and-spending -patterns-amongblack-households.htm

Wells, Terrance. (2016). Relationships between perceived racial discrimination and self-efficacy: The roles of race resilience and discrimination